SARAH WINNEMUCCA

NORTH AMERICAN INDIANS OF ACHIEVEMENT

SARAH WINNEMUCCA
Northern Paiute Writer and Diplomat

Ellen Scordato

Senior Consulting Editor
W. David Baird
Howard A. White Professor of History
Pepperdine University

CHELSEA HOUSE PUBLISHERS

New York Philadelphia

FRONTISPIECE   Sarah Winnemucca (seen here in an 1873 photograph taken in San Francisco), a member of the Northern Paiute Indian tribe, acted as spokesperson for her people. She spent much of her life helping them cope with the settlers who poured into the West in the late 19th century.

ON THE COVER   This portrait of Sarah Winnemucca, based on a photograph taken in San Francisco in 1883, shows the Paiute woman in the beaded leather dress and leggings she wore on the lecture circuit.

Chelsea House Publishers

EDITOR-IN-CHIEF   Richard S. Papale
MANAGING EDITOR   Karyn Gullen Browne
COPY CHIEF   Mark Rifkin
PICTURE EDITOR   Adrian G. Allen
ART DIRECTOR   Maria Epes
ASSISTANT ART DIRECTOR   Howard Brotman
MANUFACTURING DIRECTOR   Gerald Levine
SYSTEMS MANAGER   Lindsey Ottman
PRODUCTION MANAGER   Joseph Romano
PRODUCTION COORDINATOR   Marie Claire Cebrián

North American Indians of Achievement

SENIOR EDITOR   Liz Sonneborn

Staff for SARAH WINNEMUCCA

COPY EDITOR   Laurie Kahn
EDITORIAL ASSISTANT   Michele Berezansky
DESIGNER   Debora Smith
PICTURE RESEARCHER   Alan Gottlieb
COVER ILLUSTRATION   Maria Ruotolo

Printed and bound in Mexico.

First Printing

1   3   5   7   9   8   6   4   2

Library of Congress Cataloging-in-Publication Data

Scordato, Ellen.
Sarah Winnemucca: northern Paiute writer and diplomat/by Ellen Scordato.
   p. cm.—(North American Indians of achievement)
Includes bibliographical references and index.
Summary: Discusses the life of the Paiute woman who became known for her out-spoken criticism of the government's mistreatment of her people in the late nineteenth century.
ISBN 0-7910-1710-9
1. Hopkins, Sarah Winnemucca, 1844?–1891—Juvenile literature. 2. Paiute Indians—Biography—Juvenile literature. 3. Paiute Indians—History—Juvenile literature. [1. Hopkins, Sarah Winnemucca, 1844?–1891. 2. Paiute Indians—Biography. 3. Indians of North America—Biography.] I. Title. II. Series.
E99.P2H717 1992   92-2910
973'.0497402—dc20   CIP
[B]   AC

CONTENTS

NORTH AMERICAN INDIANS OF ACHIEVEMENT

BLACK HAWK
Sac Rebel

JOSEPH BRANT
Mohawk Chief

COCHISE
Apache Chief

CRAZY HORSE
Sioux War Chief

CHIEF GALL
Sioux War Chief

GERONIMO
Apache Warrior

HIAWATHA
Founder of the Iroquois
Confederacy

CHIEF JOSEPH
Nez Perce Leader

PETER MACDONALD
Former Chairman of the Navajo
Nation

WILMA MANKILLER
Principal Chief of the Cherokees

OSCEOLO
Seminole Rebel

QUANAH PARKER
Comanche Chief

KING PHILIP
Wampanoag Rebel

POCAHONTAS AND CHIEF POWHATAN
Leaders of the Powhatan Tribes

PONTIAC
Ottawa Rebel

RED CLOUD
Sioux War Chief

WILL ROGERS
Cherokee Entertainer

SEQUOYAH
Inventor of the Cherokee Alphabet

SITTING BULL
Chief of the Sioux

TECUMSEH
Shawnee Rebel

JIM THORPE
Sac and Fox Athlete

SARAH WINNEMUCCA
Northern Paiute Writer and
Diplomat

Other titles in preparation

ON INDIAN LEADERSHIP

by W. David Baird
Howard A. White Professor of History
Pepperdine University

Authoritative utterance is in thy mouth, perception is in thy heart, and thy tongue is the shrine of justice," the ancient Egyptians said of their king. From him, the Egyptians expected authority, discretion, and just behavior. Homer's *Iliad* suggests that the Greeks demanded somewhat different qualities from their leaders: justice and judgment, wisdom and counsel, shrewdness and cunning, valor and action. It is not surprising that different people living at different times should seek different qualities from the individuals they looked to for guidance. By and large, a people's requirements for leadership are determined by two factors: their culture and the unique circumstances of the time and place in which they live.

Before the late 15th century, when non-Indians first journeyed to what is now North America, most Indian tribes were not ruled by a single person. Instead, there were village chiefs, clan headmen, peace chiefs, war chiefs, and a host of other types of leaders, each with his or her own specific duties. These influential people not only decided political matters but also helped shape their tribe's social, cultural, and religious life. Usually, Indian leaders held their positions because they had won the respect of their peers. Indeed, if a leader's followers at any time decided that he or she was out of step with the will of the people, they felt free to look to someone else for advice and direction.

Thus, the greatest achievers in traditional Indian communities were men and women of extraordinary talent. They were not only skilled at navigating the deadly waters of tribal politics and cultural customs but also able to, directly or indirectly, make a positive and significant difference in the daily life of their followers.

From the beginning of their interaction with Native Americans, non-Indians failed to understand these features of Indian leadership. Early European explorers and settlers merely assumed that Indians had the same relationship with their leaders as non-Indians had with their kings and queens. European monarchs generally inherited their positions and ruled large nations however they chose, often with little regard for the desires or needs of their subjects. As a result, the settlers of Jamestown saw Pocahontas as a "princess" and Pilgrims dubbed Wampanoag leader Metacom "King Philip," envisioning them in roles very different from those in which their own people placed them.

As more and more non-Indians flocked to North America, the nature of Indian leadership gradually began to change. Influential Indians no longer had to take on the often considerable burden of pleasing only their own people; they also had to develop a strategy of dealing with the non-Indian newcomers. In a rapidly changing world, new types of Indian role models with new ideas and talents continually emerged. Some were warriors; others were peacemakers. Some held political positions within their tribes; others were writers, artists, religious prophets, or athletes. Although the demands of Indian leadership altered from generation to generation, several factors that determined which Indian people became prominent in the centuries after first contact remained the same.

Certain personal characteristics distinguished these Indians of achievement. They were intelligent, imaginative, practical, daring, shrewd, uncompromising, ruthless, and logical. They were constant in friendships, unrelenting in hatreds, affectionate with their relatives, and respectful to their God or gods. Of course, no single Native American leader embodied all these qualities, nor these qualities only. But it was these characteristics that allowed them to succeed.

The special skills and talents that certain Indians possessed also brought them to positions of importance. The life of Hiawatha, the legendary founder of the powerful Iroquois Confederacy, displays the value that oratorical ability had for many Indians in power.

The biography of Cochise, the 19th-century Apache chief, illustrates that leadership often required keen diplomatic skills not only in transactions among tribespeople but also in hardheaded negotiations with non-Indians. For others, such as Mohawk Joseph Brant and Navajo Peter MacDonald, a non-Indian education proved advantageous in their dealings with other peoples.

Sudden changes in circumstance were another crucial factor in determining who became influential in Indian communities. King Philip in the 1670s and Geronimo in the 1880s both came to power when their people were searching for someone to lead them into battle against white frontiersmen who had forced upon them a long series of indignities. Seeing the rising discontent of Indians of many tribes in the 1810s, Tecumseh and his brother, the Shawnee prophet Tenskwatawa, proclaimed a message of cultural revitalization that appealed to thousands. Other Indian achievers recognized cooperation with non-Indians as the most advantageous path during their lifetime. Sarah Winnemucca in the late 19th century bridged the gap of understanding between her people and their non-Indian neighbors through the publication of her autobiography *Life Among the Piutes*. Olympian Jim Thorpe in the early 20th century championed the assimilationist policies of the U.S. government and, with his own successes, demonstrated the accomplishments Indians could make in the non-Indian world. And Wilma Mankiller, principal chief of the Cherokees, continues to fight successfully for the rights of her people through the courts and through negotiation with federal officials.

Leadership among Native Americans, just as among all other peoples, can be understood only in the context of culture and history. But the centuries that Indians have had to cope with invasions of foreigners in their homelands have brought unique hardships and obstacles to the Native American individuals who most influenced and inspired others. Despite these challenges, there has never been a lack of Indian men and women equal to these tasks. With such strong leaders, it is no wonder that Native Americans remain such a vital part of this nation's cultural landscape.

Vol. 4

THE SAN FRANCISCO

No. 176

ILLUSTRATED

WASP

PUBLISHED EVERY SATURDAY.

PRICE 10 C^{TS}

OFFICE:
602 CALIFORNIA ST.
N.W. COR. OF KEARNY ST.

San Francisco, December 13 1879

RECORDED AT SACRAMENTO CAL.
BY THE PUBLISHERS OF THE WASP
PUBLISHED & STEAM PRINTING BY E. KORBEL & BROS. S^T

"ENTERED AT THE POST OFFICE AT SAN FRANCISCO CAL. AND ADMITTED FOR TRANSMISSION THROUGH THE MAILS AT SECOND CLASS RATES."

SARAH WINNEMUCCA

1

SARAH TAKES THE STAGE

The people in Platte's Hall were growing impatient. Assembled in the ornate San Francisco auditorium in November 1879, these elegantly dressed Californians were waiting to hear a most unusual speaker. Settling into their comfortable plush-covered seats, they glanced at their pocket watches, gazed at the empty stage, greeted friends across the aisles. The buzz of expectant conversation swelled.

Democratic Americans have long been intrigued by the trappings and titles of royalty, and these San Franciscans were no exception. Whetting their interest in this evening's program had been the flurry of notices around the city, promising a lecture by a genuine "princess." This princess, however, was no foreign potentate. She was Sarah Winnemucca, the daughter of a leader of the Northern Paiutes, a group of Indians who lived in western Nevada.

Whatever kind of princess she was, Winnemucca would be addressing an eager crowd. San Franciscans were curious about her people, who had been among North America's original residents. Many whites, of course, had heard frightening tales about Indians: Newly arrived easterners had described passing through Indian

The San Francisco Illustrated Wasp for December 13, 1879, front-paged the personality of the hour: Sarah Winnemucca, the 35-year-old Paiute Indian woman who was then giving lectures about the injustices suffered by her people. The costume illustrates the artist's fancy rather than its subject: Winnemucca never wore a feather headdress in her life.

11

homelands whose residents strongly resented non-Indian strangers in their area.

Most of the audience at Platte's Hall knew relatively little about Native Americans; what they did know, they had probably learned from the press. Daily papers often featured articles and first-person accounts about encounters with Indians. These stories, however, usually focused on battles between Indians and explorers, U.S. Army troops, or settlers. Uniformly written by non-Indians, they almost always portrayed Indians as enemies. Few San Franciscans had ever heard a Native American talk about non-Indians, and fewer still knew much about the Indian way of life. This audience wanted to know more.

Suddenly, the crowd stopped chattering and burst into applause: Sarah Winnemucca had appeared. Striding confidently to center stage, she wore a buckskin dress embellished with fringe. Her embroidered skirt fell just below her knees, revealing the bright scarlet leggings that modestly hid her legs; an eagle-feather headdress crowned her long black hair. Accustomed to seeing women in bonnets and long cloth skirts, the city dwellers stared in fascination at what they saw as exotic attire.

As Winnemucca began to talk, her fluency surprised some listeners; they had not expected an Indian to speak English as well as they themselves did. Never glancing at her notes, the Paiute woman spoke easily, telling stories about how her people lived, how they survived in the harsh atmosphere of the western Nevada desert, and how they raised their children. Adding a lighter touch to her address, she included humorous anecdotes and pungent imitations of people she had known. Her listeners responded warmly, sometimes sitting in total silence, sometimes roaring with laughter or spontaneously breaking into applause.

Residents and visitors stroll down Virginia City's main street in the 1880s. The boisterous Nevada community, scene of a mad scramble for silver in 1859, was also the site of the Winnemucca family's 1864 stage debut. Twenty years old when she made her first appearance before an audience, Sarah Winnemucca had become a polished professional by the time she addressed standing-room-only crowds in San Francisco in 1879.

This 35-year-old Indian woman was clearly no stranger to the stage. She had, in fact, first stepped before an audience in 1864, when she was 20 years old. On that occasion, which took place in Virginia City, Nevada, she had acted in a program of *tableaux vivants* (French for "living pictures," these are scenes of life depicted by silent and motionless people in costume).

Sharing the stage with Sarah Winnemucca had been her younger sister, known as Elma, and their father, called Old Winnemucca. After each of the tableaux, Old Winnemucca gave a short speech, which Sarah interpreted. The family's scenes included "The Indian Camp," "The War Council," "The War Dance," and "Scalping the Prisoner."

As Gae Canfield, a Sarah Winnemucca biographer, points out, the Paiutes had desperately few sources of income; they performed in such shows to provide money for their basic needs. Designed to amuse and educate non-Indian audiences, the Winnemuccas' tableaux conformed to the non-Indian stereotype of tribal existence, which was based mainly on the general public's sketchy knowledge about the Great Plains Indians. The life of these people, who inhabited the grasslands and prairies in the center of the North American continent, was actually quite unlike that of the Paiutes.

Soon after their 1864 performance in Virginia City, the Winnemuccas traveled to San Francisco to present their show at the city's Metropolitan Theater. The confident eloquence Sarah Winnemucca displayed during her 1879 speeches sprang in part from this early theatrical practice; her experience as an interpreter and emissary for the Paiutes also added to her poise. But by the time she was lecturing in Platte's Hall, Winnemucca's goal was far more serious than that of merely entertaining an audience for profit.

Haunted by her memories of the starvation and deprivation endured by her people, Winnemucca was now speaking for them. Non-Indian settlers, ranchers, and miners had been forcing the Paiutes from the reservations allotted to them by the U.S. government. The tribe had been barely able to survive on this reservation land to start with, and now even it was being stolen.

Ignoring Indian property rights, non-Indians were establishing homesteads on the choicest sections of the reservations. The "Indians' country," one federal worker had recently noted, "is passing rapidly from them. Every garden spot and tillable acre of land is now being sought out and occupied by white men. Their groves of piñon [a tree that supplied the Indians with vital food] are disappearing before the strokes of his axe, their grass-seed is consumed by his herds, the antelope and mountain sheep are killed or driven away." The interlopers had also

Old Winnemucca and his daughters Elma and Sarah gave several performances at San Francisco's Metropolitan Theater (pictured in 1865) in 1864. Trying to earn money for their needy tribe, the Winnemuccas entertained non-Indian audiences by acting out "The War Dance," "Scalping the Prisoner," and other flamboyant but inauthentic scenes of tribal activity.

started to cast their fishing nets in Pyramid Lake, a rich source of trout that had traditionally belonged to the Paiutes alone.

The federal Bureau of Indian Affairs (BIA), part of the Department of the Interior, assigned agents to safeguard the welfare of the Indians, but few did their job well, and some even stole the provisions and clothing the government issued to the Paiutes. Winnemucca had seen infants die and men and women suffer from starvation and exposure. She was determined to publicize these wrongs, hoping that her people's wretched story might move some citizens to action.

In late 1879, Winnemucca gave a series of lectures to standing-room-only crowds in San Francisco. Local and regional newspapers covered the speeches; several, including the *San Francisco Call*, the *San Francisco Chronicle*, the Nevada *Daily Silver State*, and the *Daily Alta California*, also ran feature stories about her.

A Paiute woman uses a woven-grass sieve to sort pine nuts, product of the piñon tree. A crucial part of the Indians' winter diet, the nuts became increasingly scarce as settlers relentlessly cut the piñons and planted food for themselves. "We Indians are the little fish," Winnemucca told white audiences, "and you eat us all up and drive us from home."

The San Francisco press had demonstrated a strong interest in Winnemucca from the moment she arrived; as she stepped off a steamboat from Portland, Oregon, reporters started beseiging her with personal questions. Perhaps she appreciated the attention; in any case, she gave the newspaper people a few details about her own colorful history. Her life, however, was not what she wanted to talk about. She had come to San Francisco with one purpose: to put the case of the Paiutes before the widest possible audience.

Winnemucca described the Paiutes' first contact with white explorers, which had occurred only a few years before her birth. She detailed the misunderstandings and sometimes tragic events that had followed that first meeting. She talked sadly of the government's broken promises about the reservations it had given the Paiutes, and the unequal justice it meted out to Indians. She noted that Indians were not citizens.

As her non-Indian audiences listened somberly, Winnemucca quietly asserted that her people were—and always had been—ready to negotiate in good faith with the whites who had entered their country. Some of these non-Indians, she said, had been hypocrites, professing to be pious Christians but behaving in a decidedly non-Christian way when it came to Indians.

The *Daily Alta California* reported on Winnemucca's last San Francisco speech, given in December 1879. After recording her words, the reporter added his own parenthetical asides about the crowd's reaction:

> I want homes for my people but no one will help us. I call upon white people in their private houses. They will not touch my fingers for fear of getting soiled. That's the Christianity of white people. . . .
> You take all the natives of the earth in your bosom but the poor Indian, who is born of the soil of your land and who has lived for generations on the land which the good God

"Princess" Winnemucca models the clothes and jewelry she wore during her 1879 San Francisco lecture series. The Paiutes did not really use royal titles, but lecture-hall publicists convinced Winnemucca that she would reach more people as a princess than as a plain Indian, and she finally agreed to let them bill her that way.

has given to them, and you say he must be exterminated. (Thrice repeated, with deep passion, and received with tremendous applause.)

The proverb says the big fish eat up the little fishes and we Indians are the little fish and you eat us all up and drive us from home. (The audience reacted with sympathetic cheers to this statement.)

Realizing that she had the crowd on her side, Winnemucca began to talk about positive actions that could improve the Indians' situation. Her listeners may have expected her to ask them directly for money, but instead, she spoke of ways to help the Indians help themselves. She said they particularly needed books and teachers. Educated Indians, asserted Winnemucca, would quickly become "law-abiding citizens of the United States." She completed her speech to a roar of applause and cheers.

Winnemucca was pleased with the reception she received, but she knew that helping the Paiutes would require more than stirring speeches. Before she left San Francisco in 1879, she composed a petition asking the government to protect the Paiutes' land and rights. She collected citizens' signatures on the petition, then sent it to the Department of the Interior in Washington, D.C. She departed from San Francisco knowing that for the moment, she had done as much as she could to bring the Paiutes' plight to the attention of the world outside.

Winnemucca's determination to speak out for her people would remain firm throughout her life. Her mission had led to both remarkable accomplishments and bitter disappointments in the past, and it would lead to controversy, achievements, and heartbreak in the future.

2

▾▾▾
PAIUTE CHILDHOOD

Sarah Winnemucca was born in 1844 near Humboldt Lake, in what was then called Utah Territory and is now the state of Nevada. Her mother, Tuboitonie, and father, Old Winnemucca, gave her the Paiute name Thocmetony, which means "shellflower." Thocmetony was the couple's fourth child; preceding her had been two sons, who became best known by their non-Indian names, Natchez and Tom, and a daughter who was usually called Mary. A few years after Thocmetony's birth, her sister Elma was born.

The Winnemucca family, like other members of the Northern Paiutes, lived with small bands of relatives. (Farther south lived a tribe known as the Southern Paiute. Sharing a name but little else with the Northern Paiute, these Indians lived in an entirely different way and even spoke a different language from that of the northerners.)

Thocmetony's closest relatives were prominent in their band. Her father, Old Winnemucca, led the men on antelope hunts through the desert. Her mother's father, Captain Truckee, was regarded by the tribe as its leader, although he was not a "chief" in the sense that non-Indians understood the term. Despite their limited power, however, when the Paiute leaders made a decision, few members of the tribe disputed it.

Attired in a fashionable non-Indian jacket, shirt, and tie, Old Winnemucca sits for a studio portrait in 1880. The Paiute leader, whose name means "the giver," followed tribal tradition by marrying and supporting several women. One of them, Tuboitonie, was the mother of Natchez, Tom, Mary, Elma, and Thocmetony, who was later known as Sarah.

Truckee had been one of the first Paiutes to make contact with non-Indians; it was they who gave him his English name. Until Thocmetony was five years old, her tribe's relations with non-Indians had little effect on her; her family continued to live much as the Paiutes always had.

The Northern Paiutes' homeland included the western part of present-day Nevada, southeast Oregon, and northeast California. Because the availability of water made life easier and food sources more abundant, the Paiutes centered themselves around Pyramid Lake and the Truckee River, and around Humboldt Lake and the Humboldt River a few miles to the west. The Winnemucca band lived primarily in the Great Basin, a desert to the east of the Sierra Nevada. Life in this dry region was harsh, and food sources were few.

The Paiutes depended on the natural materials available to them, and their pattern of living followed the cycle of the seasons. For food in the early spring, the Paiute women gathered the tender shoots of *tule*, a type of cattail or rush that grew in the shallow marshes near the lakes and rivers. Later in the year, they wove the dried rushes into mats to cover the round, domed Paiute homes known as *karnees*. Paiute women also harvested eggs from nests built by the birds that flocked to the marshes after the long, cold winters.

In the spring, Paiute bands from all over the Great Basin assembled at the Truckee River to spear the *cui-ui* (suckerfish) that came from Pyramid Lake. Also in the spring and again in the fall, the Paiutes gathered at the river to catch spawning salmon trout. The men speared the fish and tossed them onto the riverbank, where the women quickly cleaned them. They roasted and served some on the spot, but they dried and smoked most of them for the winter's food supply.

Thocmetony's older brother, Natchez, acquired his name through a kind of misunderstanding: Presenting him to a group of white people one day, his grandfather said, "This is my natchez"—the Paiute word for "little boy." The whites, his sister recalled in her 1883 autobiography, then "called him Natchez, and he has had that name to this day."

The rolling hills and clear lakes of Thocmetony's home-land (now part of Nevada) had provided generations of Paiutes with abundant food, but the settlers changed all that. "When the white people came into our country," Thoc-metony would recall, "they came like a lion, yes, like a roaring lion." The newcomers hacked down the Paiutes' nut trees, took over their grazing land, and wiped out the game they had depended upon.

Desert, covered with sagebrush and greasewood, stretched for miles beyond the water. Late in the hot summers, the Northern Paiutes traveled to the dry foothills of the Sierra Nevada, where piñon trees grew. From the cones of these trees, the Indians extracted pine nuts, which they stored in tightly woven tule baskets. Pine nuts were a crucial part of their food supply during the frosty winters when little grew.

Another food source was game. Armed with bows and arrows, the men hunted on foot, bringing back mule deer, pronghorn antelope, and bighorn sheep. Rabbit hunts involved the entire tribe: Forming themselves into a circle around a promising patch of sagebrush, the men would gradually move closer together, stampeding the rabbits toward a wide net where they could be quickly dis-patched. The Indians made good use of these animals,

eating or sun drying the meat and making warm clothing from the skins. The Paiutes ignored no possible source of food; they gathered grass seeds, used sticks to dig up edible roots, and even roasted grasshoppers.

As a very young girl, Thocmetony watched Tuboitonie gather food and listened to her stories. Years afterward, she described her mother's tales as "traditions of old times, even the first mother of the human race; and love stories, stories of giants, and fables." She also recalled the Winnemucca band as close-knit. "We are taught to love everybody," she noted. "Our tenth cousin is as near to us as our first cousin."

On the subject of child rearing, Thocmetony said, "My people teach their children never to make fun of any one, no matter how they look. . . . If you make fun of bad persons, you make yourself beneath them. Be kind to all, both poor and rich, and feed all that come to your wigwam. . . . In this way you will make many friends for yourself." Tribe members, she added, called the most highly esteemed women and men "mother" and "father." Recalling the cooperative nature of Paiute life, she wrote:

> The chiefs do not rule like tyrants; they discuss everything with their people, as a father would in his family. Often they sit up all night. They discuss the doings of all, if they need to be advised. . . . If the women are interested they can share in the talks. . . . The men never talk without smoking first. The women sit behind them in another circle, and if the children wish to hear, they can be there too.

> The women know as much as the men do, and their advice is often asked. . . . They are always interested in what their husbands are doing and thinking about. And they take some part even in the wars. . . . It means something when the women promise their fathers to make their husbands *themselves*. They faithfully keep with them in all the dangers they can share. They not only take care of their children together, but they do everything together.

A string of cui-ui, *a type of suckerfish found only in Nevada's Pyramid Lake, hangs drying in the sun. The Paiutes, who speared huge masses of the fish each spring, preserved most of them for use during the winter months.*

In Thocmetony's childhood, this centuries-old way of life began to alter. The changes had begun in 1844, the year of her birth, when her grandfather met a group of white explorers. Leading this 26-man exploring expedition was army captain (and later first U.S. senator from California and governor of Arizona Territory) John Charles Frémont; acting as Frémont's guide was Christopher "Kit" Carson, the legendary scout and trapper.

Exploring the dry region south of what became Oregon, Frémont, Carson, and the others were surprised to come upon a vast lake surrounded by mountains. They continued south to the mouth of a river, where they saw a large triangular rock; because it reminded Frémont of a pyramid, he named the deep body of water Pyramid Lake. When Thocmetony's grandfather and a group of other Indians entered the scene, they welcomed the whites by saying "truckee, truckee" (Paiute for "good" or "all right").

Unable to communicate with the Indians but aware that they offered friendship, Frémont exchanged salutations and gave the leader a name based on his own welcoming word: "Captain Truckee." Frémont also used the term to name the nearby river, to this day known as the Truckee.

Apparently a man of great curiosity, Captain Truckee eagerly encouraged contact with these "white brothers." He sought to learn as much about them as he could and tried to teach his band not to fear them. After their peaceful initial meeting, Truckee and Frémont became friends. When Frémont headed west later in the year, Truckee gathered 12 Paiute men, accompanied the white explorer to California, and fought alongside him as he tried to rid California of Mexican control.

In the course of the California campaign, Frémont supplied Truckee and his men with guns, ammunition, non-Indian clothing, and knowledge of the English

Members of explorer John Charles Frémont's expedition make camp at Pyramid Lake in 1844, the year of Thocmetony's birth. Amazed by the huge, pyramid-shaped rock projecting from the body of water, Frémont gave the lake the name by which it is still known.

language. Predictably, when the Indians returned home in the spring, their new weapons and clothes attracted countless questions and much admiration from their fellow Paiutes.

But when Truckee and his men returned to California in the fall of 1846, their relatives began having second thoughts about these "white brothers." Entering Paiute country had been increasing numbers of non-Indian settlers, none of them displaying the courtesy and friendship that Frémont and his explorers had shown. The Paiutes' suspicions about non-Indians increased when they learned about the ill-fated Donner party, a group of 87 California-bound settlers who in 1846 became trapped by an early blizzard in the Sierra Nevada.

To their horror, the Paiutes learned that the Donner party's 47 survivors had escaped starvation only by eating their dead. Saving themselves in this manner would never have occurred to the Indians, who now began to wonder if cannibalism was an acceptable practice among whites. The tribe's conversations about the ghastly incident went on all winter and formed one of Thocmetony's earliest, sharpest, and most terrifying memories.

During Truckee's absence, Thocmetony's father, Old Winnemucca, heard that whites were killing Indians in the Great Basin region. To escape the violence, he took his band to the mountains that summer. In the fall, however, they had to return to the Great Basin to catch fish and gather grass seed for the coming winter.

The Indians fished and collected seed in peace, as usual burying their winter supplies under a large dome made of grass and mud. But just as they finished sealing the precious dome, they detected the approach of non-Indians and quickly headed for the mountains. Tuboitonie tied Elma to her back, grabbed Thocmetony's hand, and fled with her sister and niece. Remembering the nightmarish tales of the Donner party, and realizing that their two little girls could not keep up, the desperate mothers determined to hide them. Thocmetony later recalled the scene:

> [My aunt said], "Let us bury our girls, or we shall all be killed and eaten up." So they went to work and buried us, and told us if we heard any noise not to cry out, for if we did [the non-Indians] would surely kill us and eat us. So our mothers buried me and my cousin, planted sage bushes over our faces to keep the sun from burning them, and there we were left all day.
>
> Oh, can any one imagine my feelings *buried alive*, thinking every minute that I was to be unburied and eaten up by the people that my grandfather loved so much? . . . At last we heard some whispering. . . . I could hear their footsteps coming nearer and nearer. I thought my heart was coming right out of my mouth. Then I heard my mother say, "Tis right here!" Oh, can any one in this world ever imagine what were my feelings when I was dug up by my poor mother and father?

Weeping with joy to find the girls alive and safe, their parents carried them to safety in the mountains. There, the Indians waited for the whites to clear out, but while they waited, the whites found the store of winter food and burned it. The Paiutes regarded this act as evil beyond comprehension. Deciding he could not agree with his father-in-law Truckee about cooperating with non-Indians, Old Winnemucca called a meeting of the bands in the mountains.

At the meeting, his daughter recalled, Old Winnemucca announced: "These white people must be a great nation, [but] I fear we will suffer greatly by their coming to our country; they come for no good to us, although my father [in-law] said they were our brothers, but they do not seem to think we are like them."

In the spring of 1850, Truckee decided to return to California with a large party of Paiutes. Assembling a

An 1850 photograph shows the California fishing village of Stockton as it looked when Thocmetony's grandfather Truckee took her there for a visit. Terrified by most of what she saw on the West Coast, the six-year-old girl was particularly fearful of its white residents, whom she believed to be child-eating cannibals.

group of about 30 people, he insisted that his daughter Tuboitonie and her 5 children accompany him. Old Winnemucca refused to go; he remained behind as tribal leader, probably with his second family. (The Paiute culture allowed men to have more than one wife.)

Terrified by the prospect of meeting whites on the trip west, Thocmetony rode behind her brother and, for most of the journey, hid under a robe. Truckee carried what he called his "rag friend"—a letter given him by Frémont, which he used introduce himself to the non-Indians he met on the way. At nearly every encounter, Thocmetony wept in fright and hid.

Throughout the journey, Truckee talked to his granddaughter about the non-Indian world. He tried to persuade her, she recalled, that "his white brothers and sisters were very kind to children." Her grandfather, she added, "said I must not be afraid of the white people, for they are very good. I told him they looked so very bad I could not help it." She remarked, "I would not have been so afraid of them if I had not been told by my own father and grandmamma that the white people would kill little children and eat them."

Truckee told Thocmetony that once she actually met some white people, she would lose her fear, but her first

encounter with them did not improve matters. With a hint of amusement, she described the scene in her 1883 book, *Life Among the Piutes* (as the tribe's name is sometimes spelled):

> My mother said there were two white men coming.
>
> "Oh mother, what shall I do? Hide me!" I just danced around like a wild one, which I was. I was behind my mother. When they were coming nearer, I heard my grandfather say, "Make a place for them to sit down."
>
> Just then, I peeped round my mother to see them. I gave one scream, and said, "Oh, mother, the owls!"
>
> I only saw their big white eyes, and I thought their faces were all hair. My mother said [to Truckee], "I wish you would send your brothers away, for my child will die."
>
> I imagined I could see their big white eyes all night long. They were the first ones I had ever seen in my life.

Taylor's Ferry was one of dozens that carried people, wagons, and livestock over California's San Joaquin River in the mid-19th century. Truckee's white friend Hiram Scott ran a similar operation at his riverside ranch in Stockton, where Thocmetony, her siblings, and their mother spent the summer of 1850.

Truckee told Thocmetony about non-Indians' houses, boats, and other things she could not even imagine. Finally, after they crossed the Sierra Nevada, they came to Stockton, California, on the San Joaquin River. There, Thocmetony saw one of the wonders Truckee had described—"a big house that runs on the river." That amazing house, he had said, "whistles and makes a beautiful noise, and it has a bell on it which makes a beautiful noise also." But instead of interesting her, the "house"—a steamboat—terrified the little girl, who begged to return to her father.

After a while, Thocmetony became ill, her face swollen so badly that she could not see. Tuboitonie told her father that the non-Indians had poisoned the child, but Truckee recognized the problem as nothing worse than a severe case of poison oak.

When word of Thocmetony's illness reached the local settlement, a sympathetic white woman arrived at the Indians' encampment. The woman, whose own daughter had just died, felt the need to help another child, and she patiently and affectionately nursed Thocmetony back to health. When she was sick, Thocmetony thought she was in the care of an "angel"; when she recovered and learned her nurse had been a white woman, she felt more trusting of non-Indians.

As soon as Thocmetony was well enough to travel, Truckee led his band up the river. They stopped at a ranch owned by Hiram Scott, a white man Truckee had met on an earlier trip. The rancher wanted some men to drive most of his horses and cows to the mountains to graze for the summer; he also wanted to hire some of the Indians to care for the animals that remained and to help out with cooking and dishwashing. Truckee agreed that he and a few of the other men would take the livestock to the mountains. Some of his band, including Tuboitonie, her children, and her brothers, would stay at the ranch and look after the cattle and horses there.

Tuboitonie regarded the plan with apprehension, for her adolescent daughter Mary was very attractive and had already been harassed by white ranch hands. But Truckee assured Tuboitonie that Scott would look out for their welfare, and the women remained to cook for the ranchers. It was not a happy time for them. Every night, as Thocmetony remembered, "The men whom my grandpa called his brothers would come into our camp and ask my mother to give our sister to them. They would come in at night, and we would all scream and cry; but that would not stop them."

The women soon began to leave the ranch each night to hide, but one evening, five white men tried to trap them in their tent. The Paiutes managed to escape and reach safety in a nearby boardinghouse, but they were thoroughly frightened by the experience. The next morning, Scott invited the Paiutes to his home and told them he would supply a wagon to take them to their relatives in the mountains.

In Scott's house, Thocmetony's terror gave way to intense curiosity. She was amazed by her first sight of a dining table and red, upholstered chairs, and overjoyed when she actually got to sit in one. She was, however, less enthusiastic about the beverage the whites gave her to drink. "I tasted the black hot water [coffee]; I did not like it," she said. Thocmetony was delighted at the prospect of riding in a wagon, but her sister Mary had been too distressed by her recent experience to enjoy the idea. Thocmetony later wrote of their conversation:

> I ran up to sister, and said, "Ain't you glad we are going to ride in that beautiful red house?" I called [the wagon] house. My sister said, "Not I, dear sister, for I hate everything that belongs to the white dogs. I would rather walk all the way; oh, I hate them so badly!"

The Paiutes' time in the mountains passed uneventfully. At the end of the grazing season, Truckee and his men led the livestock back to the ranch and received a handsome payment in cash and horses. On their way home to the Great Basin, Truckee lectured his people about non-Indians. "Now, my children, you see that what I have told you about my white brothers is true," he said. "You see we have not worked very much, and they have given us all horses. Don't you see they are good people?"

After many days of travel, Truckee and his group arrived in Genoa, on the western side of the Carson River. The Paiutes had passed this spot on their way to California less than a year earlier, but much had changed. Thocmetony noticed a number of brand-new buildings: a sawmill, a gristmill, and five new houses. The non-Indians were steadily taking over the Paiutes' living area.

As Truckee and his band approached their home ground, they met some Paiutes who brought news of tragedy: A typhus epidemic had killed most of their people. "They said almost all the tribe had died off, and if one of a family got sick it was a sure thing that the whole family would die," wrote Thocmetony. "[One] said the white men had poisoned the Humboldt River and our people had drank the water and died off."

Inquiring about his son, Old Winnemucca, Truckee learned he was safe; he had taken a band of Paiutes to the mountains and had been there, away from the river, for the preceding few months. When he and his group came down from the mountains, Truckee's group could hear them coming from a distance. "They were all crying, and then we cried too, and as they got off their horses they fell into each other's arms, like so many little children, and cried as if their hearts would break," wrote Thocmetony.

Tuboitonie greeted Old Winnemucca, thankful that he had survived, but her joy faded when he told her of the toll the epidemic had taken on her family: She had lost two of her sisters, their husbands, and all but one of their children. As was the Paiute custom, Tuboitonie and the other women cut off their long hair in mourning and lamentation.

Old Winnemucca's band repeated the charge about the epidemic's start: "One and all," reported Thocmetony, "said that the river must have been poisoned by the white people." At this point, Truckee stood to address his flock. His granddaughter recorded the speech:

> My dear children, I am heartily sorry to hear your sad story; but I cannot and will not believe my white brothers would do such a thing. . . . If they had poisoned the river, why, my dear children, they too would have died when they drank of the water. . . . Some of you may live a long time yet, and don't let your hearts work against your white fathers; if you do, you will not get along.
>
> You see they are already here in our land; here they are all along the river, and we must let our brothers live with us. We cannot tell them to go away. I know your good hearts. I know you won't say *kill them.*

Truckee's speech gives a clear picture of the grim predicament in which the Pauites now found themselves. No one will ever know whether the river was poisoned or not, but in truth, the Indians were suffering and would continue to suffer at the hands of ever-increasing waves of settlers. Truckee knew all too well that resistance, hostility, even a lack of cooperation with these interlopers could mean only one thing for his people: death. His words swayed the tribe, which continued to live in uneasy proximity to the non-Indian strangers.

Determined to get along with the settlers, Truckee continued his trips to the West and his work with non-Indians. At various times during the next few years,

Major William M. Ormsby, a military officer and business-man, invited Sarah (as Thoc-metony was called from the age of 13 on) and her sister Elma to move into his Genoa, Nevada, home in 1857. During the year they spent with Ormsby and his family, the Paiute girls learned to sew, cook, and speak fluent English.

Thocmetony, Mary, Tom, Natchez, and Elma—when she was old enough—went with him. Tom and Natchez once again took jobs at Scott's ranch, and the girls worked as cooks and household help for a variety of white families.

In her book, Thocmetony mentions working for a Mrs. Roach of Stockton, among others. During this time she learned English and, according to Gae Canfield, was then probably given the name Sarah when she, along with the rest of her siblings, learned about Christianity. She used the name the rest of her life.

In 1857, Thocmetony-Sarah, now 13, and her sister Elma went to live in the Genoa home of Major William M. Ormsby, his wife, and their daughter, nine-year-old Elizabeth. Ormsby, an agent of the Carson Valley Express stagecoach line and the owner of a thriving supply store, was an important man in the area. With the Ormsbys, recalled Sarah, "we learned the English language very fast, for they were very kind to us."

Sarah and Elma were fairly happy in the Ormsby home, where they provided companionship for Elizabeth, helped with the housework, and learned to sew and cook. But late in the fall of 1859, something happened that deeply shook the Indian girls' faith in their "white brothers."

It began with the murder of two white traders who had lived some 30 miles from Genoa. Bound for California and carrying a large sum of money, the men were killed as they slept by their campfire one night. When their arrow-riddled bodies were found, townspeople, not surprisingly, assumed the men had been killed by Indians. Genoa was in an uproar, and Ormsby, as an unofficial leader of the settlers, sent for friendly Paiute leaders to help.

In response to Ormsby's message, Sarah's brother Natchez and her cousin Numaga arrived in Genoa with nearly 100 men. When the Paiutes identified the arrows as those of the Washoe tribe, Ormsby demanded to see Captain Jim, the local Washoe leader. Brought to Genoa by Numaga's men, Jim conceded that the arrows belonged to the Washoe, but he maintained that his people were innocent; at the time of the murders, he said, the whole tribe had been gathering pine nuts in the distant foothills.

As instructed by Ormsby, Numaga commanded Jim to return to his tribe and bring the guilty parties back to Genoa. "Poor, poor Washoes," wrote Sarah Winnemucca;

"they went away with very sad hearts." Nevertheless, Jim returned six days later with three men, accompanied by their wives and mothers. One of the women, reported Sarah, turned to Numaga and cried out: "Oh, you are going to have my poor husband killed. We were married this winter, and I have been with him constantly since we were married. Oh, good chief, talk for him. . . . Our cruel chief has given my husband to you because he is afraid that all of us will be killed by you."

As the other Washoe women echoed the anguished wife's cry, the prisoners broke and ran. "Of course they were shot," Sarah wrote. "Two were wounded, and the third ran back with his hands up. But all of them died." She added, "Oh, such a scene I never thought I should see! The wife of the young man threw herself down on

The settlement of Genoa (pictured in 1870) proved hospitable to Sarah and her sister, who enjoyed their stay with the "very kind" Ormsby family. Of the Ormsbys and their Genoa neighbors, Sarah later wrote: "All these white people were loved by my people; we lived there together and were as happy as could be."

his dead body. Such weeping was enough to make the very mountains weep to see them. They would take the dead bodies in their arms, and they were all bloody themselves. . . . I thought my heart would break."

Sarah then overheard Captain Jim talking to Numaga, and what she heard only increased her horror. "It is true what the women say," he confessed. "It is I who have killed them. Their blood is on my hands." Just as the young wife had asserted, Jim had given up three innocent men to prevent the non-Indians from massacring the whole tribe.

Major Ormsby, as an agent of the Carson Valley Express stagecoach line, depended upon men such as these wheelmakers in Genoa, Nevada, for the prosperity of his business.

That winter, after Natchez had escorted his sisters home, the Paiutes learned the rest of the story: Not long after the three Washoes had been gunned down, Genoa authorities discovered that the traders had been killed in a gambling dispute. To make it appear that Indians had done the bloody deed, the assassins had placed arrows in the dead men's wounds. Two white men had been captured, found guilty of the murder, and hanged.

The non-Indian community apparently felt that justice had been served, but the Indians could not share that sentiment. The Washoe incident severely strained their trust in the settlers, and tension rose through the winter. From what the Paiutes had learned about the ways of non-Indians, they had good reason to fear what the future had in store.

3

TWO WORLDS CLASH

Sarah's cousin Numaga, also known as Young Winnemucca, served as the Paiutes' war chief, but his heart yearned for peace. In 1860, however, a new outbreak of interracial violence made war inevitable, and Numaga went into battle. A brilliant military man when circumstances forced him to fight, he led the Paiutes to a string of victories in the Pyramid Lake War of 1860.

Old Winnemucca, who had camped at Pyramid Lake during the harsh winter of 1859, was delighted by the return of Sarah, Elma, and Natchez. Their account of the tragic events at Genoa, however, left him deeply troubled; he was now more sure than ever that the presence of non-Indians in Paiute lands could do his band nothing but harm.

That presence was expanding with frightening speed. Following the 1859 discovery of the Comstock Lode—one of the richest silver deposits ever unearthed—at Virginia City, immigrants swept into the area in record numbers. Many of these newcomers, Old Winnemucca observed sadly, headed for Honey Lake and seized the choicest Indian land for their own homesites. Where the Paiutes had once led antelope hunts, the settlers established their fields. Where the Paiutes had harvested pine nuts, the settlers chopped trees for firewood, gradually destroying the piñon groves so crucial to the Indians' winter food supply.

The settlers not only took the Paiutes' grazing land for their own livestock, but often stole the Paiutes' animals as well. Far worse, some settlers respected the Indians themselves no more than they did their animals. They regularly raped Indian women they found alone and sometimes killed Indian men with no provocation.

39

Old Winnemucca occasionally talked of resisting the intrusive whites, but his father-in-law always disagreed: Truckee believed that resistance meant death. Despite the pain, the thefts, the killings, the countless indignities, Truckee continued to insist that his people treat the whites as brothers.

Soon after his grandchildren's return, Truckee took sick; with a sense of profound shock, Sarah realized he was dying. The Paiutes ignited huge bonfires on the mountaintops, transmitting the grievous news to scattered members of the tribe. Heeding the signal, reported Sarah, "Our people gathered from far and near." Shortly before his death, recalled Sarah, Truckee sent for "a dear beloved white brother of his, named Snyder." The old leader asked the white man to take Sarah and Elma to California, where rancher Scott had promised to enroll them as students at the Roman Catholic mission school. After receiving Synder's oath that he would honor the request, Truckee lapsed into unconsciousness. The family watched over him as great numbers of Paiutes assembled.

An encampment of Paiute karnees, each pierced by a central stovepipe, stands amid the tailings (mining residue) at the Ophir silver mine in Virginia City around 1860. The dark squalor of the Paiutes' post-settler existence formed a cruel contrast to the green freedom they had enjoyed when the land belonged only to them.

At midnight the next day, the old man awoke and asked to be left alone with Tuboitonie, Old Winnemucca, and his grandchildren. His son-in-law raised him up as he spoke his last words: "Now, son, I hope you will live to see as much as I have, and to know as much as I do. And if you live as I have you will some day come to me. Do your duty as I have done to your people and your white brothers." Then, after asking to be buried with his "white rag-friend"—the precious letter from Frémont—he breathed his last. Sarah described the scene of grief that followed:

> Every one threw themselves upon his body, and their cries could be heard for many a mile. I crept up to him. I could hardly believe he would never speak to me again. . . . I felt the world growing cold; everything seemed dark. The great light had gone out. I was only a simple child, yet I knew what a great man he was. . . . I knew how necessary it was for our good that he should live.

True to his word, Snyder saw to it that Sarah and Elma went off to school. In the spring, he watched Natchez and five other men accompany the girls as they departed for San Jose, California. There, Scott fulfilled his own promise, enrolling the Paiute youngsters in the community's Catholic school for girls. Sarah, intelligent, curious, and proud, was excited by the opportunity, but her hopes were soon crushed by the same kind of racial prejudice that threatened the Paiutes back in Utah Territory: Within three weeks, non-Indian parents complained so vehemently about the presence of "savages" in their daughters' school that the nuns asked the girls to leave. Scott sent them back to Pyramid Lake on a stagecoach.

Meanwhile, trouble had started brewing at home. It began in January 1860, when rancher Jack Demming, one of two brothers who shared a log house north of

Honey Lake, left home to buy supplies. When he returned, Demming found his brother Dexter dead, apparently murdered by Indians. Residents of Honey Lake valley generally feared and mistrusted Indians, but Jack Demming hated them with a passion. After Dexter's death, his brother and some like-minded settlers wanted to hunt down and slaughter all the Indians—particularly Paiutes—they could find. (Their attitude may seem extraordinary to Americans of the late 20th century, but in 1860 it was all too ordinary.)

In the end, the settlers sent for Captain William Weatherlow, leader of the 60-man Honey Lake Rangers. Weatherlow was well acquainted with many Paiutes, especially with Old Winnemucca and Sarah's cousin Numaga. The captain knew that the tribe had signed a treaty with the settlers not long before the killing of Dexter Demming, and he knew they had never broken its terms.

Weatherlow believed that the murder was the work of the Pit River Indians to the far north, a tribe the Paiutes had helped the settlers repel the previous year. Arguing for the Paiutes' innocence of the Demming murder, the captain talked the settlers out of making war on them. Still, the atmosphere—among Indians and non-Indians alike—remained tense and fearful.

In the spring of 1860, Paiute bands gathered as usual on the shores of Pyramid Lake, where they planned to harvest tule shoots, spear and roast the spawning fish, net geese, and feed their ponies on the new grass. In the old days at the lake, women and men had happily worked and gossiped together after the hardship of the winter, but this year things were different. The leaders of the various bands held a council, where the talk was of matters more momentous than marriages and births, hunting and fishing. The prevailing sentiment among

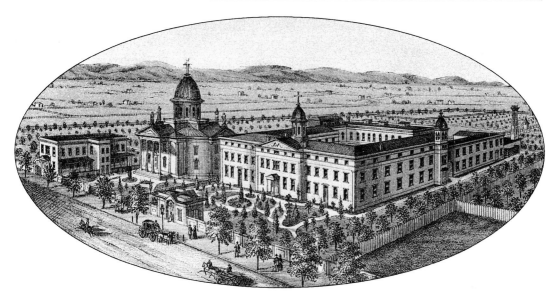

The Roman Catholic nuns at the Academy of Notre Dame in San Jose, California (pictured in the 1880s), welcomed Sarah and Elma, but the parents of the other students did not. After a series of outraged parental protests about the admission of these two young "savages," the nuns reluctantly dismissed the girls, who returned to Pyramid Lake by stagecoach.

the leaders was anger; most wanted to drive the non-Indians from Paiute lands by armed force.

Numaga, the group's young war chief, disagreed vehemently. He went from family to family, speaking eloquently and at length against war. When the people stood firm, he lay on the open ground and fasted, taking neither food nor water for three days. When that failed to change the other Paiutes' minds, Numaga addressed the council members again. He was just beginning to win them over when a messenger arrived with horrible news.

More murder had been done. Two young Paiute sisters had recently gone out to gather roots and had not returned when expected. Following the girls' trail, their alarmed family came to the house of the Williams brothers, two white men who owned a whiskey shop and trading post on the Carson River. The traders said they knew nothing of the sisters.

A few days later a Paiute man got into a dispute with the Williamses. In the heat of the argument, the white men set their dog on the Indian, who began shouting in Paiute. Then, from somewhere in the house, he heard

Captain William M. Weatherlow, who believed that Indians as well as settlers deserved justice, represented the best of the nation's western military: His cool head and faith in the Paiutes' word prevented a massacre after the Dexter Demming murder in 1860. Not even Weatherlow, however, could avert bloodshed when Paiutes killed two white men who had kidnapped and abused two Paiute girls.

faint answering cries in his own language; he realized he had found the lost children. Leaping onto his horse, he galloped to the Paiute camp, gathered the girls' relatives, and returned to the Williams house.

Frightened by the appearance of this band of angry Paiutes, the Williams brothers opened a trap door, which led to a hidden cellar. The girls' father descended and discovered his terrified daughters—bound, gagged, bruised, and lying on a filthy cot in the darkness. The father tore the rags from his children's mouths, heard the terrible story of their captivity and abuse, and brought them upstairs. Almost blinded by horror and rage, the Paiutes shot and killed the abductors, then set their house afire.

After listening to the messenger's report of this latest violence, Numaga knew war was inevitable. If his people were not driven to it by the settlers' actions, the settlers would be driven to it by the killing of the Williams brothers. Grimly, Numaga prepared for war.

He was, of course, correct. Word soon spread: "The bloodthirsty savages," said one report, had "murdered two innocent, hardworking, industrious, kind-hearted settlers." Sarah's old friend Major Ormsby hastily rounded up an army of settler volunteers, and the Pyramid Lake War of 1860 began. Sarah, along with the rest of the Paiute women, children, and old men, stayed safely away from the fighting, probably in the mountains.

Numaga proved himself a brilliant tactician, defeating the non-Indians in one battle after another. After three months of war (during which Ormsby was killed), the non-Indians agreed to a cessation of hostilities. At the peace talks in August, Numaga pointed out that the Paiutes would not have gone to war without provocation. Colonel Frederick W. Lander, the settlers' military representative, had learned about the events leading up to the war; he was forced to agree that some of the settlers had acted despicably.

Numaga then arranged for a meeting between Old Winnemucca and BIA agent Frederick Dodge at a place called Big Meadows on the Humboldt River. There, Dodge agreed to establish Paiute reservations on the Indians' homeland. In a letter to his superiors in Washington, D.C., Dodge enclosed rough maps of what would become the Pyramid Lake and Walker River reservations.

Believing that their lands were all their own again, the Paiutes rejoiced. They were also pleased with the appointment of Warren Wasson, an old friend of Winnemucca and Numaga's, as the reservations' Indian agent.

Bureau of Indian Affairs (BIA) agent Frederick Dodge understood that Indians, faced with the loss of their traditional hunting and fishing grounds, had two choices: to fight for their rights or to starve to death. To provide a third alternative, Dodge persuaded the federal government to set aside two vast tracts of land—Pyramid Lake and Walker River—as Indian reservations.

Truly concerned about the Paiutes, Wasson fought for their rights, but in early 1862, he left the reservation to work as a U.S. marshal. After that, the Paiutes were often without an agent; the Civil War was raging, and government officials had little interest in the welfare of the western Indians.

Most of the new agents who did appear proved incompetent or interested only in their own gain. They failed to protect the reservation from the many threats that faced it: Non-Indians pastured their livestock on the best Indian land, using up all the fresh grass and demolishing the Paiute supply of grass seed; unscrupulous traders tricked the Paiutes out of what little they had; non-Indians fished in Pyramid Lake.

Then, along with settlers and miners, a new threat to Paiute land arose. During the early 1860s, the Central Pacific Railroad began to lay track eastward, and the Union Pacific to lay it westward. In 1869, the two would connect the East and West Coasts of the nation by effecting a junction at Promontory, Utah, close by the Paiute reservation. Railroad construction, of course, would bring hordes of workers who could be expected to need huge quantities of firewood for heating and cooking.

Indian agents could not—or would not—protect the Paiutes' timberland, much of which was "acquired" (actually stolen) by greedy non-Indian traders. At about this time, white squatters seized the particularly fertile land in the Big Bend of the Truckee River, in the middle of the Pyramid Lake reservation. As Washington bureaucrats wrangled about the fine points of governing and financing the reservation system, the Paiutes found themselves living in an undefined legal situation—and acute misery.

Although the Indian agents were paid to deliver cloth, food, and farming implements to the Paiutes, they consistently failed to do so, reported Sarah Winnemucca. She also recalled that the government had promised to build the Paiutes a lumber sawmill and a gristmill to grind grain, but that the mills "were never seen or heard of by my people, though the printed report in the United States statutes . . . says twenty-five thousand dollars was appropriated to build them. Where did it go?" She wondered, "Is it that the government is cheated by its own agents who make these reports?"

Warren Wasson's appointment as Indian agent delighted his old friends among the Paiutes, but unfortunately, he proved so effective that they lost him: When tales of Wasson's decisiveness and courage reached the ears of Abraham Lincoln in 1862, the president made him U.S. marshal for the whole Nevada Territory.

Eighteen years old in 1862, Sarah Winnemucca was quite well traveled and could read and write—skills unknown to many people of all races at this time and place. But despite her education, she was an Indian, and her means of making a living were therefore sharply limited: She could work as a cook, housemaid, or seamstress. She took several such jobs in towns around Pyramid Lake, but she always kept abreast of developments on the reservation. With sorrow, she noted that the ever-increasing influx of settlers was reducing the Paiute food supply to almost nothing.

The plight of the wretched, hungry Paiutes also tormented Old Winnemucca, who felt responsible for his people's well-being. Casting about for ways to make money to feed them, he came up with with an odd—and most uncharacteristic—plan: He would go on the stage. In the summer of 1864, he designed an entertainment-education act, lined up bookings in Virginia City and San Francisco, and asked his daughters Sarah and Elma to join him in the theatrical venture.

Many people who knew the Paiutes were appalled by Old Winnemucca's move. One woman wrote to a local newspaper, bemoaning the reduction of these Paiutes to posturing, as she put it, "like savages" in order to survive. But however well-meant, the white woman's indignation did nothing to feed the Paiute people. The stage show, unfortunately, did little more; the Winnemuccas returned to the Great Basin area with much less than they had hoped for.

That part of Utah Territory became Nevada, the 36th state in the United States of America, before the end of the year. Although the settlers were delighted, the news failed to cheer the Paiutes, who looked forward to another hard winter.

Sarah went to live and work in an Indian camp in Dayton, Nevada. Her father tried to keep up the old

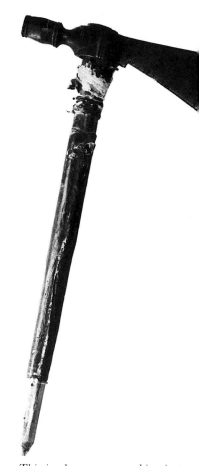

This implement—a combination peace pipe and tomahawk—was one of Numaga's most treasured possessions. In 1862, he gave it to his friend Wasson "as a sign of peace and friendship."

patterns—hunting and fishing with his wives and children around Pyramid Lake—but that way of life was increasingly difficult to maintain. At about this time, the U.S. Army set up forts along the Nevada stagecoach route to guard it against possible attacks by Confederate soldiers. The soldiers' needs, added to those of the railroad workers and ever-growing bands of settlers, further depleted the Paiute food supply. Finally, a tragedy brought the situation to a head.

In March 1865, a group of white ranchers accused the Pyramid Lake Paiutes of stealing their cattle. Galloping out from Fort Churchill went a column of Nevada Volunteer Cavalrymen, led by Captain Almond B. Wells. As the company passed through Dayton, a wave of fear and foreboding swept over Sarah; the troops were boasting that they would kill anyone they found in their way. "The days after they left," she wrote, "were very sad hours, indeed."

The Central Pacific Railroad (left) meets the Union Pacific at Promontory, Utah, on May 10, 1869. The historic moment symbolized the uniting of America's East and West Coasts; unfortunately, it also represented major trouble for the Paiutes, whose land was soon overrun with railroad men and those who supplied their needs.

Sixty miles away, in the early hours of March 17, Wells and his men came to the Paiutes' spring encampment at the reservation's Mud Lake. At the camp were the band's women, children, and old men; Old Winnemucca had taken the young men on the spring antelope hunt. At Mud Lake, the women were gathering tule shoots, waterfowl eggs, and the other foods of spring.

At 3:00 A.M. Wells and his men rode into the encampment and slaughtered every adult in sight. They saved the babies, sleeping in baskets—for last. Before they left, the soldiers set the camp on fire and threw the baskets into the flames to watch them burn. Tuboitonie, Old

Maguire's Opera House (left rear) in Virginia City was the scene of the Winnemucca family's stage debut in 1864. Their appearance prompted some sympathetic responses— one white woman wrote to a newspaper, expressing regret that the proud Paiutes had been forced to act "like savages" for their living—but it failed to produce any substantial revenue for the desperate Indians.

Winnemucca's other wife, and Sarah's infant half brother probably died at Mud Lake. Mary escaped on horseback, but she was the only survivor. When Old Winnemucca returned to what had once been his people's peaceful camp, he found 32 charred corpses amid the still-smoldering wreckage.

Mary died later that year, possibly in another raid, when the non-Indians went on a rampage, killing any Indian they discovered outside a reservation or town. The tone of a report in the *Humboldt Register*, a local newspaper, suggests the non-Indians' general sentiments about the Paiutes: "The boys rode through the Indian ranks, scattering and shooting down everything that wore paint." Among the dead were "80 warriors and 35 squaws," noted the newspaper writer. "The latter were dressed the same as the bucks, and were fighting—and had to be killed to ascertain their sex."

Choosing not to fight alongside the men, Sarah's sister Elma left Nevada and went to Marysville, California. She was soon adopted by a family of French immigrants, and later married a white man named John Smith. Old Winnemucca fled to the mountains to the northwest, leaving his son Natchez at the Pyramid Lake reservation and Sarah living in Virginia City. Sarah, who agonized over the breakup of her family, must have found it unbearable to live among the people who had massacred her mother and relatives. In 1866, determined to help what remained of her people, she abandoned Virginia City and went to live with Natchez at Pyramid Lake.

Deprived of their traditional means of survival, the Paiutes were forced to depend on Indian agents, those government employees assigned to manage the reservations and supply their residents with food, clothing, and other necessities. During her first winter at Pyramid Lake, Winnemucca had a series of disturbing encounters with one of these agents, a man named Nugent. This official, who charged the Paiutes for the government supplies he was supposed to give them, had made himself, not surprisingly, extremely unpopular on the reservation.

In 1866, Winnemucca reported that she, Natchez, and his wife "got along very poorly, for we had nothing to eat half of the time." Occasionally, agent Nugent allowed the women to do his laundry; in return, wrote Winnemucca, "he would give us some flour to take home." In 1867 Nugent sold some gunpowder to a Paiute man, thereby violating federal regulations. After leaving Nugent's quarters, the Paiute met another white man—one of the Indian agent's employees—who shot him dead for carrying the forbidden gunpowder.

After the murder, reported Winnemucca, "All our people were wild." Planning to take revenge by shooting both Nugent and the killer, a party of enraged young warriors ignored Natchez's pleas for calm and set out for the agent's home. "What shall we do?" the young man asked his sister. "We will go and tell [Nugent and his friend]," she responded, "to go away this very night." At that, sister and brother leapt onto their horses and sped off to Nugent's, almost drowning on the way in a rain-swollen river.

When Winnemucca and her brother arrived, breathless and bedraggled, Nugent scornfully dismissed them. Then he called to his men. "Get your guns ready," he shouted gleefully. "We will show the damned red devils how to fight!" As it turned out, the vengeful young warriors had ridden not to Nugent's but to the nearby settlement of Deep Wells, where they fatally wounded two white men. When Nugent learned of the raid, he fled in terror to Camp McDermit, a U.S. Army fort a few miles distant.

Late that night, a messenger brought Winnemucca a letter from the fort. Obviously assuming that she was in

RENO, NEVADA

An 1860s lithograph offers a bird's-eye view of Fort Churchill, base of Captain Almond B. Wells and his team of Nevada Volunteer Cavalrymen. One of the darkest moments in western American history occurred at 3 A.M. on March 17, 1865, when Wells and his men rode into the Paiutes' Mud Lake encampment, slaughtered every Indian in sight, then burned the camp

charge of her people at the reservation, it said: "Miss Sarah Winnemucca—Your agent tells us very bad things about your people's killing two of our men. . . . I want to talk to you and your brother." The letter was signed "Captain Jerome, Company M, 8th Cavalry." Resourcefully using a pointed stick and fish blood to scrawl a reply, Winnemucca promised to get there as soon as possible, gave the note to the messenger, and saddled two horses.

"We were soon on the road to see the soldiers," Winnemucca recalled. "We went like the wind." Waiting at the fort were both Nugent and Jerome. Winnemucca told the officer the whole story, beginning with Nugent's sale of the gunpowder, his aide's murder of the Indian, and the warning she and Natchez had delivered. She also described a few earlier incidents, such as the kidnapping of the two little girls in Genoa and the massacre at Mud Lake. Jerome listened to her recital in silence. When she finished, he quietly told her not to be afraid. He said she should return to the reservation, where he would join her the following day.

True to his word, Jerome arrived the next morning. Obviously shocked and moved by the Paiutes' misery on the reservation, he immediately ordered his men to deliver three wagonloads of army food and clothing, which arrived two days later. "Oh, how glad we were," Winnemucca wrote. "That was the first provision I had ever seen issued to my people!" At that point, Nugent sidled up to Jerome and said, "If you want to issue beef to the Indians, I have some cattle I can sell you." Jerome ordered him off the reservation.

After feeding the starving Paiutes, Jerome questioned Winnemucca and her brother, then asked if they could find their father—who was off in the distant mountains—and persuade him to join them. If Old Winnemucca would bring all his people to the fort, said Jerome, he would see to it that the army fed and supplied the whole tribe. "Sarah, don't cry," he said. "You and your brother shall go with me, and . . . you will be cared for by the officers of the army."

Some of the Paiutes, understandably, regarded Jerome's proposal with suspicion. "Maybe they will kill [your father]," friends told Winnemucca. "You know what liars the white people are, and if you go and get him and he is killed by the soldiers, his blood will be on you." But Winnemucca and Natchez trusted Jerome, and they decided these military men had nothing to gain from mistreating the Paiutes.

Indeed, reasoned Winnemucca, it was to the army's advantage to keep the Indians peaceful. Unlike the Indian agents who profited by withholding stores from her people, most of the U.S. Army officers at Camp McDermit felt, as Winnemucca heard one of them put it, that "it was easier to feed Indians than fight hungry ones."

In July 1867, Natchez left the reservation to find his father. Sarah Winnemucca remained at Camp McDermit and in 1868 accepted a position as interpreter at the fort, where she felt she could best help her people. Some of the Paiute women fought alongside their men in battle, but Winnemucca chose to avoid armed skirmishes. She was determined to fight for the Paiute with her own weapons: her intelligence, her education, and her knowledge of the non-Indian world.

Fort McDermit (seen in an 1887 photograph) became a welcome refuge for Sarah Winnemucca and her people in 1867. After spending a miserable winter at Pyramid Lake with the corrupt Indian agent Nugent, the Paiutes found McDermit's officers both generous and honest.

4

"I WANT YOUR PROTECTION"

In July 1868, a year after he had set out to find his father, Natchez brought Old Winnemucca and 490 of his people into Fort McDermit. There, the Paiutes were fed well and treated far more kindly than they had been on the reservations. Nevertheless, some of the Paiutes—understandably, considering the long history of non-Indian betrayal of Native Americans—still mistrusted all non-Indians, including the soldiers.

Bands of Indians on their own not only frightened settlers and ranchers but put themselves in danger; even in the late 1860s, many non-Indian Nevadans felt perfectly justified in shooting any roving Indians they saw. Partly for this reason, the army tried to gather as many Paiutes as possible into military locations: Fort McDermit, Camp Smith, or Camp Harney, an outpost in Oregon.

Technically, the army classified the tribes as prisoners, but Sarah Winnemucca, who was on the military payroll as a scout, believed her people were better off under the army's protection than that of reservation Indian agents. Some of the Paiutes failed to understand her position, complaining that she was getting rich—she earned $65 a month—at their expense. A crisis at the Pyramid Lake and Walker River reservations, however, silenced these critics.

Soon after Winnemucca began working at McDermit, an outbreak of measles—a European illness against which the Indians had no natural resistance—struck the Pyramid Lake Paiutes, killing at least 100. That same year, another 100 Paiutes, weakened by poor living conditions and hunger, died at Walker River from tuberculosis, typhoid fever, and other illnesses. At that point, many Paiutes came to agree with Winnemucca that they were better off under the army's care. Hundreds followed her into the army camps.

Winnemucca, now 24 years old, had already laid down some ground rules, which eased the adjustment of the incoming Paiutes, especially the women and girls, to life at the camp. She explained her move in *Life Among the Piutes*:

> After my brother had gone, I went to the commanding officer, and said, "Colonel, I am here all alone with so many men [and] I am afraid. I want your protection. I want you to protect me against your soldiers, and I want you to protect my people also; that is, I want you to give your orders to your soldiers not to go to my people's camp at any time, and also issue the same order to the citizens." Accordingly, the order was issued . . . and the result was that we lived in peace.

Winnemucca strove to help not only her own band but all the Paiutes. In 1868, for example, overcrowding became a serious problem for the 400 Paiutes living at Camp Smith. "There was no game in that region of any kind," noted Winnemucca, "except now and again a hare. [The Indians] had no land to cultivate, but were living on anything they could do or gather."

Fearing an outbreak of violence from the hungry tribe, the area's non-Indians asked the military to transfer the Paiutes to the much larger Fort McDermit, 65 miles

Old Winnemucca and his band, who had fled the anti-Indian violence at Pyramid Lake in 1865, rejoined Sarah at Fort Mc-Dermit in 1868. Shortly after their arrival, 400 more Paiutes, escorted by Sarah, moved from overcrowded Camp Smith to McDermit, bringing its Indian population to 900. Technically classifying them all as prisoners, the army managed to provide plentiful food and decent living accommodations.

distant. The army agreed to the change, and at the request of McDermit's commander, Winnemucca and her half brother Lee (one of Old Winnemucca's sons by his second marriage) went to Smith, gathered the Paiutes together, and escorted them to Fort McDermit.

At the new post, now home to some 900 Paiutes, the Indians enjoyed much-improved living conditions. "Every head of a family was furnished with a good tent of the requisite size for his family," Winnemucca noted with satisfaction. "Every morning, at five o'clock, rations for the day were issued. A pound and a half of meat was given to every grown person, and good bread . . . and once a month coffee, rice, sugar, salt, pepper, and beans were issued. . . . Every one had enough. . . . It is this generosity and this kind care and order and discipline that makes me like the care of the army for my people." The army, however, could care for the Paiutes only when they were technically prisoners, and the army camps were not equipped to provide for hundreds of prisoners indefinitely.

The Civil War had ended in 1865. In its aftermath, during the fall of 1868, President Ulysses S. Grant began appointing military officers to posts formerly held by civilians. Among them was the new Indian superintendent for Nevada, Major Henry Douglass. As soon as he arrived in Nevada, Douglass—who believed that the government owed the Indians justice and decent treatment—set about learning the exact situation of the tribes in his territory. During the winter, he wrote to an officer at Fort McDermit, inquiring about the status of the Paiutes there. On April 4, 1870, he received a reply, which had been written by Sarah Winnemucca.

Winnemucca's thoughtful and thought-provoking letter astonished and impressed Douglass, who sent it to friends and coworkers in Washington, D.C. The missive created a minor furor in the East: Washingtonians copied,

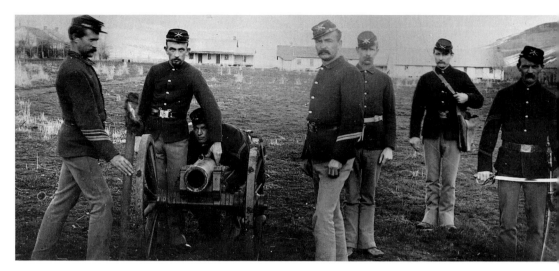

distributed, and talked about it; *Harper's Weekly* magazine published a paraphrased version of it; New York and Boston philanthropists and reformers wrote letters to newspaper editors, enthusiastically praising the young Paiute woman and her letter.

A rare photograph from the late 1860s shows a group of soldiers on duty at Fort McDermit. The Paiutes and the military got along well; as Sarah Winnemucca observed, the army had discovered it was "easier to feed Indians than to fight hungry ones."

Word of Winnemucca's new admirers soon reached the West, where most residents viewed all Indians with scorn. Settlers resented easterners who seemed to care more about Indians than about non-Indians; and one newspaper editor in Boise, Idaho, in fact, directed a torrent of abuse at Winnemucca. Referring sarcastically to the beauty of this "Indian Princess," he suggested it could be improved by more frequent washing and the use of a comb. Next, training his sights on Sarah's gentle father, the editor said Old Winnemucca was famous for cutting out settlers' tongues, stealing their horses, and making war on innocent ranchers.

Glorified in the East, reviled and lied about in the West, Winnemucca had temporarily become the object of heated controversy. Interestingly, however, neither those who praised her nor those who sneered at her ever bothered to investigate the facts of her situation or even to meet her face-to-face.

Indian superintendent Douglass was different; he visited Fort McDermit to speak with Winnemucca in person. Later recording his impressions of her, he wrote: "She is a plain Indian woman, passably good looking, with some education and possessed of much natural shrewdness. She converses well." Douglass seemed surprised at Winnemucca's willingness to take a place in two worlds—that of her people and that of the non-Indians, who seemed determined to destroy the Indians. "She conforms readily to civilised customs," he wrote, "and will as readily join in an Indian dance."

After meeting Winnemucca and other friends of the Paiutes, Douglass went to work improving the Pyramid Lake reservation and restricting it to the Paiutes alone. First, he expelled the fishermen who had by this time stretched more than 20 nets across the Truckee River. Next, he drew up plans to improve the Paiute reservations and those of other Indian groups in Nevada. He had just begun to execute those plans when bad news arrived from Washington, D.C.: President Grant had relieved him of his duties as Indian superintendent.

Grant, in fact, had dismissed all army officers in such positions and announced that all Indian agent jobs would now be filled by members of the American Baptist Home Mission Society. In her research, biographer Gae Canfield discovered that Douglass, genuinely dedicated to the Paiutes, had left detailed notes and instructions about the tribe for his successors.

Among Douglass's papers was the information that he had never received a map accurately describing the boundaries of the Walker River reservation, a lack that caused him great difficulties in disagreements with non-Indian squatters. And the dismissed superintendent firmly pointed out that Nugent, the agent with whom Winnemucca and Natchez had had such trouble, had rented the use of the reservation's grasslands to cattle

more expensive to the government to restore order and quiet
after the Indians have once broken out, and it does not require
much provocation to make them do so. I know more about
the feeling and prejudices of these Indians than any other
Person connected with them + therefore I hope this petition
will be received with favor. Sir I am the daughter
of the Chief of the Pirites I am living at Camp
McDermit and have been in this employ of the U.S.
government for nearly three years as interpeter and
guide. I have the honor to be, Sir, your
                        most obedient Servent
                        Sarah Winnemucca
                        Camp McDermit Nev

PS   please answer this short Epistle
if you consider me worthy and
I promise you that my next letters
will be more lengthy Derict to
Camp McDermit Nev
                        Sarah Winnemucca
                        Augst 9th 1870

ranchers. Nugent did very well—the cattlemen paid $1
for each head of cattle they grazed, leaving Nugent a
personal profit of $15,000. That money, said Douglass
emphatically, should have been used to improve the
reservation and feed and clothe the Paiutes.

Winnemucca felt deep concern about the removal of
Douglass, but in 1870 she had concerns of a more personal
nature: She had fallen in love. The object of her affection
was Edward C. Bartlett, a Fort McDermit officer who

Dated August 9, 1870, Winnemucca's gracefully penned note to a BIA official demonstrates her mastery of English. An earlier Winnemucca letter, written to Henry Douglass, had earned its writer a throng of non-Indian admirers.

returned her feelings. Because Nevada law forbade marriage between Indians and whites, the couple eloped to Salt Lake City, Utah, where they were married on January 29, 1871.

At the age of 27, Winnemucca may have decided she deserved a little personal happiness and seized it in her own energetic fashion, but her choice proved unfortunate. Old Winnemucca and Natchez despised Bartlett, and his bride soon learned why. Although she had lived at Fort McDermit, she had not discovered that Bartlett was an alcoholic, a man well known for irresponsible behavior. Biographer Canfield reports that on one occasion, for example, the fort's commanding officer had left Bartlett in charge. After an evening of heavy drinking, Bartlett jumped on his horse and started galloping through the fort, screaming that the Paiutes were about to attack. (The Paiutes had never attacked an army base; besides, there was not a Paiute in sight at the time.)

Bartlett's fellow officers seemed willing to tolerate his antics, but Winnemucca was not. She was outraged when, in Salt Lake City, she discovered he had taken the jewelry she had bought as an investment, pawned it, and then spent the money. She was also shocked to learn that her husband was absent from his post without leave. The situation quickly became unbearable, and within a few weeks, she sent for Natchez, who traveled to Salt Lake City and accompanied her home.

Winnemucca returned to her job at Fort McDermit, and renewed her concern with the Paiute reservations. In March 1871, Baptist minister George Balcom arrived to take charge of the Pyramid Lake reservation. Well-meaning but incompetent, Balcom used federal Indian funds to build and stock a schoolhouse—when what the Paiutes desperately needed was food. The new agent was both confused by his unpopularity and further troubled by Nugent.

Nugent and a number of non-Indian area residents had deeply resented Indian superintendent Douglass and his efforts to help the Paiutes. They were especially irate about the dam he had built, which, they believed, threatened their fishing on the reservation's rivers. Perhaps looking for a kind of secondhand revenge on Douglass, Nugent persuaded some of the angry local men to dress as Paiutes, surround Balcom's house, and terrify him into leaving. The maneuver worked; Balcom soon resigned, to be replaced as Walker River Reservation agent by another Baptist, C. A. Bateman.

By the time Bateman arrived, Winnemucca's impatience with the government's operation of the reservations had boiled over; she had written to the BIA, sharply criticizing both Balcom and Bateman. Meanwhile, Bateman began to investigate conditions at Pyramid Lake; what he found was not encouraging. With the reservation food supply virtually nonexistent, many Paiutes had left the reservation in disgust. After explaining, in a letter to Washington, that the Paiutes who remained had been "criminally neglected," Bateman ordered a large shipment of food and clothing for them. Unfortunately, the supplies failed to arrive, prompting Winnemucca to fire off another salvo of stinging criticism.

Throughout 1872 and into 1873, Winnemucca remained at Fort McDermit. The camp seemed less attractive to her, however, after her ill-fated marriage, and in late 1873 she moved 80 miles south to the town of Winnemucca, named after her father. There she rented a room and took on sewing jobs to support herself.

During this period, Winnemucca also worked as a translator for Captain Dodge, an agent for the Shoshone people. Assisting him one day as he distributed government supplies to the Shoshones, Winnemucca was surprised to note the appearance of Bateman, the Paiutes'

Winnemucca, pictured in one of the outfits she designed for her lectures, made a favorable impression on Indian superintendent Douglass in 1870. "She is a plain Indian woman, passably good looking, with some education and possessed of much natural shrewdness," wrote Douglass. "She converses well."

agent. She was even more surprised when Bateman provided the Shoshones with one ton of flour, foodstuff desperately needed by the hungry, destitute Paiutes.

Winnemucca was appalled. Was Bateman trying to impress Dodge? That, she did not know, but she did know her people were in far greater need than the Shoshones, and she knew she was furious. Marching up to Bateman, she lit into him as the bewildered Dodge looked on. "You come up here to show off before this man," she shouted. "Go and bring some flour to my people on Humboldt River, who are starving, the people over whom you are agent. For shame that you who talk three times a day to the Great father in Spirit-land should act so to my people." Leaving Bateman openmouthed, the disgusted Paiute woman stormed back to the town of Winnemucca.

Meanwhile, Natchez remained at Pyramid Lake. He got along badly with Bateman, who blamed him for stirring up trouble among the few Paiutes still at the lake. Old Winnemucca had fled to the Steens Mountains in southern Oregon, and several other bands of Paiutes had also chosen to abandon the reservation. Now, deciding that the situation at Pyramid Lake was getting out of his control, Bateman told Natchez to leave as well. "You and your sister talk about me all the time," Natchez reported Bateman as saying. "I don't want you and your sister here." Angrily, Natchez responded, "This is my reservation, not yours. I am going to stay here just as long as I like."

Enraged by Natchez's refusal to leave voluntarily, Bateman plotted to remove him by other means. He wrote a letter asserting that Natchez had behaved illegally, told the illiterate Paiutes it was a request for clothing for them, and obtained their marks, or signatures, on the bottom of the missive. The scheme worked: Federal authorities soon arrested Natchez and sent him to prison on the island of Alcatraz in San Francisco Bay.

Winnemucca was naturally aghast at this mockery of justice—and she was not alone. A number of influential non-Indians who had dealt with Natchez had developed great respect for him. As outraged by his unjust imprisonment as Winnemucca was, these friends used all the influence at their command to regain freedom for the young Paiute leader; in February 1874, they succeeded.

When Natchez returned, he and Winnemucca got in touch with Old Winnemucca and persuaded him to accompany them on an important mission to San Francisco. Having received better treatment from the U.S. Army than from BIA agents, the Winnemuccas hoped to arrange for the military to take permanent charge of the Paiutes. Paying a call on General Schofield, the Pacific area army chief, the three Indians made their request. Schofield appeared sympathetic, but he pointed out that the army could not simply usurp the duties of a federal agency. Because such a switch could be mandated only by the U.S. Congress, Schofield urged the Winnemuccas to see the Nevada senator.

The Winnemuccas took Schofield's advice and visited the senator. He listened to their plan, gave them a $20 bill for the trouble they had taken to see him, and told them he would do what he could to help. Apparently, however, he failed to bring the Paiutes' plight to the attention of Congress; in any case, nothing came of the Winnemuccas' visit.

The Pyramid Lake reservation remained a shambles. Finally, Indian commissioner A. C. Barstow visited the reservation to settle a dispute about land with the Central Pacific Railroad. What he saw shocked him. Almost all the Paiutes had left the reservation. For those few who had stayed, there were no houses. Nor did they have a teacher, a preacher, or an agent. Bateman had abandoned

Winnemucca's brother Natchez shows off an army badge, probably the gift of a soldier friend at Fort McDermit. When he received a call for help from his usually self-reliant little sister in 1871, Natchez rushed to Salt Lake City and carried Winnemucca away from her new husband, Edward Bartlett, who had proved both a drunkard and a thief.

Pyramid Lake for Sacramento, California, although he continued to draw his salary. Barstow's visit resulted in Bateman's forced resignation. Yet his replacement, A. J. Barnes, proved even worse. He blatantly stole goods meant for the Paiutes.

Desperate to help their people, Winnemucca and her father went to beg for food at Fort McDermit. Sadly, the mission accomplished nothing: McDermit's commander said he could neither issue the Paiutes supplies nor house them as prisoners, as had happened six years earlier. Deeply disappointed, Sarah Winnemucca returned to the town of Winnemucca, and her father went back to southern Oregon, which had become his refuge.

At the same time, Natchez and his family settled in Lovelock, Nevada. Eventually, millionaire Leland Stanford, one of the era's more spectacular politicans and railroad tycoons, presented the young Paiute man with 160 acres in Lovelock. The acreage provided the pleased Natchez with more than enough space for hunting and fishing.

Winnemucca was not nearly as lucky. Some of the whites in Winnemucca presumed that, as an Indian woman in a non-Indian town, she must be a prostitute, and they physically accosted her in the street. She responded to one particularly threatening assault by drawing a knife and superficially wounding the man who had been harassing her. The incident landed Winnemucca in jail for a night. On another occasion, she got into a brawl with a white woman who had verbally abused her.

Despite Winnemucca's unhappy situation, she was determined to carry on and to help her people. Her optimism may not have been very well founded; yet she soon saw an opportunity present itself from an entirely unexpected direction.

Camp Harney, Oregon (pictured in 1872), became the temporary home of Old Winnemucca and his tribe in the spring of 1875. Sarah joined her father at Harney in May, but a few months later, she persuaded him to accompany her to the Malheur Reservation, where she had signed on as an interpreter.

5

BEGINNING AGAIN

In May 1875, Sarah Winnemucca traveled to Camp Harney, Oregon, where her father and his band had stopped after leaving their winter encampment. The Paiutes' world had undergone radical change over the previous three decades; long gone were the days when the tribe gathered at the Truckee River to catch the early cui-ui run. Still, Old Winnemucca clung to a few remnants of tradition, and family members continued to meet in the spring.

At Camp Harney, Sarah listened to the usual tales of the births, deaths, and marriages that had taken place over the winter. One day, in the middle of such a conversation, Sarah's half brother Lee came to the camp with a message for her about another reservation for the Paiutes.

Malheur Reservation (also known as Malheur Agency), about 50 miles to the east of Camp Harney, had been established 3 years earlier and was now being run by Indian agent Sam Parrish. Lee told his half sister that Jarry Lang, a cousin on their father's side, had been Parrish's interpreter. Lang's eyesight had deteriorated from disease, however, and Natchez had sent him to San Francisco for treatment. In the meantime, Parrish needed a new interpreter and wanted to hire Winnemucca. Lee told Sarah that she ought to take Lang's place.

Despite her initial hesitation about becoming rein-volved with reservation affairs, Winnemucca agreed to become Parrish's interpreter, but only after Old Win-nemucca consented to go with her to Malheur. The job paid her $40 per month, and with Parrish renting her a room for $15 a month, Winnemucca found her financial situation greatly improved. She then focused on Parrish's attitude toward the Paiutes in his care.

Parrish proved entirely different from the other agents with whom Winnemucca had dealt. He told the Paiutes that the reservation land belonged to them and that the government would pay them for the crops they raised. Sincerely interested in the Paiutes' welfare, Parrish constantly urged them to become self-sufficient farmers. Winnemucca recorded one of his first speeches to the tribe:

> I have come to show you how to work, and work we must.
> . . . I will try and do my duty, and teach you all how to
> work, so you can do for yourselves by-and-by. We must
> work while the government is helping us, and learn to help
> ourselves. . . . Now you see the government is good to you.
> It gives you land for nothing, and will give you more—that
> is it will give you clothes, and a store, and I want you,
> chiefs of the Piutes, to ask all your people to come here to
> make homes for themselves. . . . This is the best place for
> you all.

With little room in the increasingly settled West for bands of hunters, the U.S. government had decided to encourage Indians to farm on their reservations. For centuries, the Northern Paiute had lived by hunting, fishing, and harvesting wild crops. But even though they had never been farmers, many were willing to give the government's plan a chance.

Among those assembled at Malheur was Oytes, leader of a band of traditional hunters from an area to the east. Oytes and his followers had looked down on all the Paiute groups, including Old Winnemucca's, that did not have

Sam Parrish, the Indian agent assigned to the Malheur Reservation in Oregon, liked and respected the people under his care; the Paiutes, in turn, gave the agent their trust and loyalty.

a history of hunting on horseback. And they had no interest whatever in farming. "I have my men, and our father Winnemucca has his," Oytes told Parrish. "I am not going to work. I and my men have our own work to do—that is, to hunt [for food] for our children."

Parrish conceded that Oytes and his men should keep to their own ways. But the other bands—including those of Old Winnemucca and of a leader called Egan—agreed to learn to farm. Parrish assigned them plots of land and seeds for potatoes, turnips, watermelons, barley, oats, and hay.

One of Parrish's first moves was to ask the cooperative Paiutes to dig an irrigation ditch. The result impressed Winnemucca, who later noted wryly that the ditch was "two and a half miles long and ten feet wide. . . . They were only six weeks at it. This is quite a contrast to our Pyramid Lake Reservation. They only got three miles of ditch on that reservation, which is twenty-three years old. They have been building a dam and a ditch all this time." Once the ditch was under way, Parrish began to select individuals to learn various trades: He taught three men blacksmithing, another three carpentry, and assigned others to build a road.

Among Parrish's other projects was a schoolhouse. He planned to build a new structure at Malheur and install his sister-in-law as the teacher, with Winnemucca serving as her assistant. He also intended to build a flour mill and asked the government for funds and supplies. The Paiutes appreciated this energetic, good-hearted man. They worked comfortably with him, even when he urged them to adopt certain non-Indian ways. When he saw old men and women working in the fields, for example, he told the women to go home and cook for their families—which seemed very odd to the Paiutes, whose women had always been in charge of foodstuffs. Nevertheless, they complied with his request. Parrish commanded the loyalty and affection of all the Paiutes—except for Oytes's band.

The following fall, when a group of Columbia River Indians arrived to trade with the Paiutes, Oytes seized the opportunity to continue his old ways. Because the members of this tribe had earned a reputation as troublemakers, Parrish wanted no part of them; he forbade the newcomers to enter Malheur. Oytes and his band promptly traveled to the Columbia River Indians' camp about 30 miles away to trade with them. When he returned to Malheur, he announced that he intended to live permanently among the Columbia River Indians.

By now, Oytes had begun to anger Parrish. When a shipment of government goods arrived a short time later, the agent distributed it to all the Paiutes except for Oytes and his band. (Winnemucca noted approvingly that for once, everything sent for the Indians' use was given—not sold—to them.)

Deeply insulted that Parrish should have slighted him in front of his own men, Oytes now threatened to kill him. Like many of the Paiutes, Winnemucca was deeply afraid of Oytes because he was a shaman, a religious figure who claimed to possess magical powers. Oytes, in fact, went so far as to boast that an arrow could not harm him. Deciding to call his rival's bluff, Parrish told him, "Oytes, I have three hundred dollars. If you will let me shoot at you, if my bolt won't go through your body the money is yours. You say bolts cannot kill you." But Oytes would not say it again; he refused Parrish's deal and thereby enabled the agent to gain even greater stature among the Paiutes.

Parrish further pleased the Paiutes by allowing them to keep a large portion of the crops they had raised on plots he had assigned to each family. Formerly, the agents had taken most of the crops away, insisting that they belonged to the government in payment for use of the

Obligingly conforming to the non-Indian concept of an "Indian Chief," Old Winnemucca wears an ornate military uniform, a feather headdress, and a nose ornament in this formal portrait from the 1860s.

land. More than a few of the agents had been known to sell the produce and keep the proceeds for themselves.

Throughout the winter, the Paiutes worked on finishing the irrigation ditches and the schoolhouse. Then news came that the non-Indians in nearby Canyon City were claiming that the Paiutes had not been making good use of the land. The Canyon City residents wanted the western end of Malheur Reservation to be placed under their own control.

The suggestion met instant opposition from the Paiutes. "We don't want to give up any of our reservation," said Egan, one of the leaders. "The Pyramid Lake

Reservation is too small for us all, and the white people have already taken the best part of it. . . . Another thing, we do not want to have white people near us. We do not want to go where they are, and we don't want them to come near us. We know what they are, and what they would do to our women and our daughters." Parrish backed the Paiutes—and earned the enmity of the Canyon City residents. Nevertheless, the Paiutes kept the land.

In the spring of 1876, Jarry Lang returned from California nearly blind and unable to support his wife and family. Allowing him to resume his job as interpreter, Winnemucca became an assistant teacher at the newly opened schoolhouse. To her surprise and delight, she greatly enjoyed teaching, especially after she started instructing the Paiutes in their own language rather than in English.

Her idyll would not last. One of the Canyon City residents, displeased by the Paiute holdings and resentful of Parrish, lodged a complaint against the agent to his

An Indian agent (right center, wearing black derby hat) presides over the distribution of supplies to a band of Paiutes near Burns, Oregon, around 1900. Although some agents performed their jobs honestly, Winnemucca discovered that all too many grew rich by keeping or selling the goods earmarked for tribal use.

superiors. Apparently, the grievance did the trick. Word soon arrived at Malheur that Parrish was to be replaced.

Winnemucca, her father, Egan, and even Oytes—who had learned to regard Parrish with respect—journeyed to Camp Harney to see if the officers there could help them. But nothing could be done, and on June 28, 1876, W. V. Rinehart arrived to take over the agent's duties. A strict and fervent Baptist and former army officer, Rinehart was notorious for his violent temper. The Paiutes resented him from the start, both for replacing the popular Parrish and for addressing them in a haughty, disciplinarian manner.

Two days after Rinehart arrived in Malheur, he was joined by his family and employees, who included the reservation's new schoolteacher, Frank Johnson. Winnemucca recalled the arrivals as "the poorest-looking white people I ever saw"—but within a week, she noted, they were all wearing new clothes. The garments, she observed, bore a suspicious resemblance to the government-issue clothing Parrish had distributed to the Paiutes.

Rinehart incurred the immediate distrust of the Paiutes when he announced that the reservation belonged not to them but to the government, which would pay them $1 per day for working it. Parrish had told them something entirely different. But with Rinehart in charge, the Paiutes had little choice but to agree to work for these pitiful wages.

At the end of the week, the Paiutes arrived at the agent's house to be paid. Before he handed out their wages, Rinehart explained that he had deducted the cost of the clothing and rations the Indians had been issued, and that they could use the remaining money to buy goods at the government store. He said nothing about the disposition of the crops the Paiutes were raising.

The Indians began to realize that Rinehart had no intention of letting them keep the crops. And without the harvest, they feared, they would starve. They had, moreover, become accustomed to receiving clothing and rations without exchanging cash. Speaking for his fellow Paiutes, an angry Egan addressed Rinehart. Winnemucca recorded his words:

> Why do you want to play with us? We are men, not children. We want our father [the government] to deal with us like men. . . . Don't say you are going to pay us money, and then not do it. . . . We did not ask you to pay us. . . . You did not say anything about the clothing nor about what we ate while we were working. . . . Sam Parrish sent for those things which are in the store for us, and you want us to pay you for them. You are all wearing the clothes that we fools thought belonged to us, and we don't want to pay you anything.

Rinehart responded to Egan's speech with a furious outburst: If the Paiutes did not like his ways, he shouted, they could all leave the reservation. The Indians found the agent's tirade insulting, but they were even more disturbed about the possibility of being expelled from the land. Winnemucca was particularly incensed because of her insider's view: She had accompanied Parrish as he guided Rinehart around the reservation and explained how it was set up. At the time, Rinehart had seemed to agree with everything Parrish said about the Paiutes and their rights to the land and its crops.

When Winnemucca recounted the exchanges between the two agents, the other Paiutes grew silent. Then they began to ask questions. Few could fathom why Rinehart would have changed his mind, and some even wondered if Winnemucca had told the truth about the conversations between Parrish and Rinehart. Their whisperings made her feel that her reputation had been tarnished, a matter of grave importance to her.

Winnemucca soon saw a frightening demonstration of Rinehart's temperament. One day, she observed him ask a little boy to find Jarry Lang and bring him to his office.

W. V. Rinehart, the harsh, hot-tempered Indian agent who took over the Malheur Reservation in 1876, withheld the Paiutes' crops, mistreated their children, and threatened his critics with expulsion from the reservation. When Winnemucca led her people in lodging a formal complaint against the tyrannical agent, she lost her job as reservation interpreter.

The boy giggled, sending the agent into a paroxysm of violent rage. He slammed the child's ear with his closed fist, then threw him to the ground and kicked him savagely and repeatedly. The agent finally turned to the horrified Winnemucca. "I won't have any of the Indians laughing at me," he snarled. "I want you to tell them that they must jump at my first word to go. I don't want them to ask why or what for." Winnemucca tried to explain that the child spoke no English, but the agent ignored her. Anyway, he had made himself clear: The little boy died from the beating.

Rinehart's temper showed itself time and again. One day, for example, Winnemucca told him that Lee and his men had just arrived from Pyramid Lake and wanted to buy rations. Rinehart told Johnny, a young Paiute boy who worked for him, to open the storehouse. Instead of racing to obey, Johnny made an impertinent remark to his boss, then pretended he could not perform the task. Such casual behavior from an Indian made Rinehart see red. He seized his pistol and announced he would shoot the little boy. Terrified, Johnny took to his heels. "Of course, that is the kind of men that are called good," observed Lee, "men who talk to the Spirit Father three times a day, but who will kill us off as they would kill wild beasts."

Catching up with Johnny, Rinehart handcuffed him, told him he would be hanged for disobedience, and locked him up. The boy's distraught mother begged for his life, but Rinehart paid no attention. Then he turned to Winnemucca with a sly smile and whispered that the boy would not be hanged but merely taught a lesson by a night alone in jail. Although she was relieved by this news, Winnemucca was still left aghast by Rinehart's cruelty.

On another occasion, Rinehart beat an Indian nearly to death for being slow to carry out a command. When the Paiute raised his hand to fend off yet another blow, Rinehart aimed his pistol at him. The near-victim was saved by a group of Rinehart's men, who pointed out that he could get in trouble for shooting every Indian who displeased him.

The situation at the aptly named Malheur (the French word meaning "misfortune") became progressively worse. Desperately needed supplies failed to arrive, although Rinehart insisted he had ordered them. The tribe members came to believe that the supplies had indeed been ordered and had arrived, but that the agent had kept them for himself. When Winnemucca, at Egan's urging, complained to the agent, he told her that if the Indians did not like the way the reservation was being run, they should go live with the army. This time, the Paiutes took Rinehart at his word. "We started for Camp Harney the next morning," Winnemucca recalled.

At the camp, Winnemucca wrote later, she led a delegation that "told the commanding officer everything about our *Christian* agent's doings, and he told me to write to Washington, and he would do the same." She penned a petition, had it signed by all the Paiute leaders at Malheur, and sent it to the nation's capital. "Then our Christian agent discharged me from my office of interpreter," she wrote in her memoirs, "for reporting to the army officers, for which I don't blame him."

By this time, Winnemucca had finally obtained a divorce from Edward Bartlett, and on November 3, 1876, she took another husband. In a ceremony at the Carson City, Nevada, home of Sam Parrish's brother Charles, Winnemucca became Mrs. Joseph Satwaller. Right after her marriage, Winnemucca attempted to return to the reservation, possibly to introduce her new husband. Rinehart refused to allow her within Malheur's bounds.

With that, Winnemucca broke her connections with the reservation. The groundwork of trust laid by Parrish

A Paiute woman gathers tule shoots, probably at Pyramid Lake. Such time-honored practices began to die out as settlers steadily encroached on the land that the Paiutes had once believed theirs for eternity.

had been destroyed, along with all her hopes for progress. She apparently moved to Oregon and settled into her new life with Satwaller, far from the scene of her bitterest disappointments. Unfortunately, her marriage to Satwaller proved a disappointment as well. By early 1878 Winnemucca was on her own again, this time doing housework for a woman who lived on Oregon's John Day River.

Before the year was out, however, Winnemucca would return to the Paiutes—under circumstances quite different than she had ever imagined.

An 1849 drawing shows Fort Hall, one of numerous military bases built to protect non-Indians passing through the Great Basin. The army's imprisonment of a large group of Bannocks at Fort Hall eventually led to the Bannock War of 1878, a bloody uprising in which the Indians suffered heavy losses.

6

THE BANNOCK WAR

I n the winter of 1878," Sarah Winnemucca wrote, "I was living at the head of John Day's river with a lady by the name of Courly. On the 21st of April I had some visitors from the Malheur Agency." Three members of her tribe had traveled north to bring her a grim message: The Paiutes were starving.

The tribe, said the three emissaries, wanted Winnemucca to go to Camp Harney and persuade army officials to file a complaint about Rinehart with his superiors. The Indians even suggested that Winnemucca travel all the way to Washington, D.C., to speak for them.

Winnemucca reminded the travelers that neither her earlier visit to Camp Harney nor her plea to a U.S. senator had done the Paiutes any good. She was, she told the three Paiutes, powerless; it would be useless for her to go to the camp or the capital.

At the end of May, another group of Paiutes arrived, twice the size of the first. The situation at Malheur Reservation had worsened, they told Winnemucca. Rinehart, enraged by their complaints, had driven a band of Paiutes from the agency. They had settled about 25 miles away, near a river where they could catch salmon. The fish was all they had to live on.

Also living along the river were some 15 Bannock Indian families, refugees from trouble at their own reservation near Fort Hall. The Bannocks' difficulties had begun when two white men raped a Bannock woman. In retaliation, the woman's male relatives had shot and killed the rapists. Hoping to prevent further violence—and, as usual, assuming it was the Indians who started it—the army had rounded up the Bannocks, confiscated their horses and guns, and restricted them to the reservation. Afraid that they, too, would be disarmed and imprisoned, the 15 Bannock families had gone to live with the exiled Paiutes.

Winnemucca, who quickly understood that the situation spelled potential trouble for all the tribes in the area, agreed to return to the Paiutes and to do what she could to help them. While living in Oregon, she had done well for herself and had managed to buy her own team of horses and a wagon. She knew, however, that she would not be earning any money while aiding the Paiutes, so she agreed to take three passengers with her on the trip to Malheur and charged them $20.

The small group set out on June 4. When Winnemucca arrived at Malheur, Egan and Oytes met her, immediately called a council, and invited the Bannocks who had escaped the army's dragnet to take part. Egan introduced Winnemucca to the Bannocks by saying: "She has done everything in her power for us and our praying agent discharged her for no other cause than that Oytes and I took her to Camp Harney to report him. Therefore you need not be afraid to talk to her. She is our friend. Tell her all your troubles. I know she will help you."

Jack, the Bannock leader, asked Winnemucca to "talk on paper" for his tribe, meaning that he wanted her to write down the events that led to the Bannocks' problems and send the account to government officials in Washington, D.C. According to Jack, the Bannocks had turned over to the authorities the two tribe members who had shot the whites. But that had not appeased army officials, and they imprisoned all the Bannocks at Fort Hall. Rumors had since begun to spread that the army planned to slaughter every tribe member at the fort.

Egan concluded the council by calling for the Paiutes to take up a collection that would send Winnemucca to Washington, D.C., to discuss the matter with the appropriate officials. All told, $29.25 was collected. "This was indeed very little to start with," Winnemucca noted, although the sum grew when the three people she had transported from Oregon to Malheur promised to pay her $50 to be taken to Silver City, Idaho.

The small party set out on June 8, the day after the council ended, and headed for the town of Elko, Nevada, where Winnemucca hoped to sell her team and wagon

Bannock warriors Buffalo Horn (extreme left) and Buffalo Jim (second from left) confer with fellow fighters before the 1878 war. Working for the U.S. Army—with a Bannock price on her head—during the conflict, Winnemucca rode hundreds of miles, often at great personal risk. "It was," she said, "the hardest work I ever did for the government in all my life."

for enough money to pay for the trip east and back. For three days, the travelers encountered no one else as they passed over rough roads that were eerily quiet. Mounting the crest of a hill near Fort Lyon, Winnemucca finally learned the reason for the lack of traffic. A man rushed to meet the wagon and to explain, Winnemucca wrote later, that "the greatest Indian war that ever was known" was then in progress. The Bannocks, said the messenger, "were just killing everything that came in their way," including the last stagecoach driver to travel along the road. The man also said that because some Paiutes had sided with the army against the Bannocks, the Bannocks had a special goal. They wanted "nothing better," said the informant, "than to kill Chief Winnemucca's daughter."

Winnemucca urged her horses on. Shortly before midnight, she reached Fort Lyon, where she was met and interrogated by a Captain Hill. Minutes after Hill questioned her, army scouts escorted a Paiute man into the captain's quarters. Rapidly firing questions at the newcomer, Winnemucca learned that the Bannocks, enraged by the army's treatment, were waging an all-out war.

Meanwhile, a few of the non-Indians at Fort Lyon who were terrified by the conflict approached another officer, Captain Bernard, and claimed that Winnemucca's wagon was full of ammunition she was conveying to the Bannocks. When Winnemucca heard this, she wrote later, "My heart almost bounded into my mouth." She immediately walked up to Bernard and said, "Go and see for yourself, captain, and if you find anything in my wagon besides a knife and fork and a pair of scissors I will give you my head for a football." Moved by her assurance and dignity, the officer took her at her word.

Afterward, Winnemucca proved her good faith by offering her services to the army for the duration of the war. Bernard promised to telegraph the commander in the region, General Oliver Otis Howard, to see if her help was needed. In the meantime, he left for Sheep Ranch, a nearby camp. Under the dangerous circumstances, his journey could not have been very pleasant. But Winnemucca's night at the fort was just as nerve-racking. The people were still suspicious of her and insisted on putting a guard on the wagon in which she slept.

The next morning, June 12, five men—four Paiutes and one white—arrived with a message for Captain Bernard from Fort McDermit. When they were told that the captain had moved on to Sheep Ranch, Winnemucca asked if she could accompany the Paiute messengers in their search for Bernard. Captain Hill gave her a horse and saddle, and Winnemucca rode 30 miles with the men at full gallop to Sheep Ranch. There Bernard asked Winnemucca if she could persuade the Paiutes to track the hostile Bannocks in the area around Malheur Reservation. The Paiutes told her it was too dangerous, then added that the Bannocks had reportedly captured and killed her brother Natchez. Immediately, Winnemucca announced that she was willing to track the Bannocks, even if she had to do it alone.

Early the next day, Captain Bernard asked Winnemucca to fulfill a request from General Howard and bring the Paiutes from Malheur to the army camp. Howard wished to protect the Paiutes—and to prevent any of them from joining the Bannocks. Accompanied by two Paiutes, Winnemucca set off for Malheur. On the second day of their journey, they reached Barren Valley, where they found the smoking remains of a ranch house the Bannocks had just burned down.

Noticing a trail heading toward Steens Mountains, Winnemucca determined that it had recently been traveled by Paiutes. She and her two escorts rode along the trail for about 60 miles. Near Juniper Lake they found a clock, a fiddle, and household goods. These items appeared to be the spoils of war, discarded by the Bannocks.

Five miles farther on, Winnemucca saw two men running down a mountain slope. She called to them, and as they approached she recognized one of them as her half brother Lee. After greeting her, he confirmed Winnemucca's darkest fears. "Oh dear sister," he said, "you have come to save us, for we are all prisoners of the Bannocks. They have treated our father most shamefully. . . . We are all up in the mountains with them." Winnemucca's heart fell at the news that her father and the rest of the tribe were being held captive, then rose when Lee told her Natchez was still alive.

Upon being told of General Howard's message for the Paiutes, Lee informed Winnemucca that delivering it would be extremely dangerous: "They have said they will kill everyone that comes with messages from the white people, for Indians who come with messages are no friends of ours, they say every night." When Winnemucca pointed out that the Bannocks would not recognize who she was, Lee told her that Oytes would; he and his band had gone over to the Bannocks' side.

Deciding that she had to take the chance of being recognized, Winnemucca started up the rocky mountain slope with the four men. When they reached its summit and looked into the next valley, she saw hundreds of Paiute tents scattered among the hostile Bannocks. Lee successfully sneaked her into the camp and led his half sister to her father's tent.

Old Winnemucca greeted his daughter with great joy, but she felt there was no time to spend on such pleasantries. "I have come to save you all," she announced, "if you will do as I wish you to and be quiet

General Oliver Otis Howard lost his right arm as a Union officer in the Civil War. After serving as commissioner of the Bureau of Refugees, Freedmen, and Abandoned Lands from 1865 to 1874, he commanded federal troops in several Indian uprisings, including Chief Joseph's War of 1877 and the Bannock War of 1878. Of Winnemucca's work as a scout and guide, Howard said, "She did our government great service."

about it. Whisper it among yourselves. Get ready tonight, for there is no time to lose, for the soldiers are close by. I have come from them with this word: 'Leave the hostile Bannocks and come to the troops.'. . . Father, you tell the women to make believe they are gathering wood for the night, and while they are doing that they can get away."

At nightfall, while the women were making their getaway, Winnemucca, her father, and six male cousins crept out of the Bannock camp and started over the rocky crest. Meanwhile, Lee secretly drove as many horses as he could to Juniper Lake. At the lake, the escapees formed a column and set off into the night. Lee, however, went back to help the remaining Paiutes find their way out of the camp.

At daybreak, the column stopped at a spot called Summit Springs, and Winnemucca finally managed to get some sleep—her first in two days. A short time later, an exhausted Paiute rode up to say that they were being followed by Bannocks. Apparently, Oytes had discovered what was going on, sounded an alert, and captured Egan and his band. The messenger was not sure what had happened to Lee.

A fearful Winnemucca decided to ride ahead and convince General Howard to protect her father's band. On the morning of June 15, she and Lee's wife, Mattie, set off on their quest. They covered 75 miles of desert before finding any water, exchanged their tired horses for fresh ones at a river crossing two hours later, then continued on at a wild gallop. "We whipped our horses every step of the way till we were met by the officers," Winnemucca recalled.

After meeting with the two women, General Howard enlisted a company to find the Paiutes and escort them safely back. At last, Winnemucca could rest. After riding about 230 miles in less than two days, she had saved her father's band. It was, she wrote later, "the hardest work I ever did for the government in all my life."

But Winnemucca's work was not yet done. The next day, the general asked her and Mattie to serve as interpreters, scouts, and guides. Through late July, the two women accompanied Howard and proved invaluable because they knew the country well—far better than the civilians who hired themselves out to the army.

On one occasion, the other scouts reported that an armed party of Bannocks were stationed 15 miles away, preparing for a battle. Winnemucca expressed strong doubts; there were probably no Indians within 200 miles, she said. As Howard and his men rode on, the soldiers noted what looked like a large number of Indians on a hill; the general, disregarding Winnemucca's statement, sent his troops to investigate. She and Mattie "just laughed," Winnemucca recalled, "for we knew what was coming." Indeed, the scouts had fallen prey to a well-known Indian ruse: By piling rocks on the crest of a hill to resemble human figures, Indians were able to attract their pursuers to one area while riding off in another direction.

During their travels with Howard, Winnemucca and Mattie observed several battles between the army and the Bannocks. After one encounter, they found an abandoned Indian infant and arranged for the girl's care. On another occasion, Winnemucca found a scalp at an abandoned Bannock encampment.

On July 27, Winnemucca and Mattie received a new assignment. They were attached to General Forsythe's company and assisted with the task of picking up small bands of hostile Indians. One day, near Granite City, Winnemucca met Sam Parrish and experienced a tearful reunion. Her sorrow increased when she learned that the Umatilla Indians had banded with the Bannocks and, in

General James W. Forsythe, commander of an army company during the Bannock War, assigned Winnemucca and her sister-in-law Mattie the job of helping to round up small, separated groups of Bannock allies. While thus engaged, Winnemucca learned that her old friend Egan, who fought for the Bannocks, had been ambushed and killed, probably for the $2,000 reward that had been offered for his scalp.

the course of their campaign, murdered Egan and then defiled his corpse by cutting it into pieces.

After traveling with Forsythe to the Steens Mountains, Winnemucca and Mattie rode on to Camp McDermit, where Old Winnemucca's band had settled. His daughter rode into the Paiute camp at dawn and woke up the first group she saw by shouting, "Here, you are sleeping too much; get up." When Natchez spied her, he shouted to his lookouts, "I am afraid, my young men, you are not doing your duty; for I have here in my camp a warrior who has just arrived." Old Winnemucca and Lee were overjoyed to see the two women, especially since they had heard tales of their being killed in a skirmish with the Bannocks.

Winnemucca continued to work with the army through the fall. As the season wore on, the Bannocks were being soundly defeated, rounded up, and sent to Camp Harney. In the camp, Winnemucca managed to find the parents of the abandoned Bannock infant and reunited them with their child.

In October, the U.S. government ordered all the Paiutes who belonged on Malheur Reservation to leave Camp McDermit and gather at Camp Harney before being sent back to Malheur. It was very sad news because it meant that Old Winnemucca and his band, who had never settled at Malheur, were to remain at Camp McDermit and become separated from the other Paiutes. After consultation with the tribe, Winnemucca appointed Leggins to serve as chief of the band being sent to Malheur. Most of the Paiutes did not want to return there because Rinehart was still in charge.

The Paiutes who remained at Camp Harney were still stationed there when winter came. Wondering when she and the others would be sent to Malheur, Winnemucca spoke with the camp commander. He had very bad news.

The federal government determined that any Indians who had been involved in the Bannock war must be removed from the area, no matter whether they had been hostile or friendly. The commander told Winnemucca that, according to a presidential order, all the Paiutes at Camp Harney were to be sent north across the Columbia River, to the Yakima reservation.

Winnemucca was aghast. "What for?" she asked. Only Oytes's band had fought with the Bannocks, she pointed out. Her arguments prompted the commander to send a letter to President Rutherford B. Hayes, pointing out the injustice of the decision. The official word came one week before Christmas. The Paiutes had to go to Yakima, far from their home.

"What!" Winnemucca protested. "In this cold winter and in all this snow, and my people have so many little children? Why, they will all die. Oh, what can the President be thinking about? Oh, tell me, what is he? Is he man or beast? Yes, he must be a beast; if he has no feeling for my people. . . . I have never seen a president in my life and I want to know whether he is made of wood or rock, for I cannot for once think that he can be a human being. No human being would do such a thing as that—send people across a fearful mountain in midwinter."

The winter march proved brutal. Constant snow caused the travelers to proceed slowly; several of them succumbed to the cold. When the band reached Yakima in early January, they were put in the care of the agent, Father James H. Wilbur. "We were turned over to him as if we were so many horses or cattle," Winnemucca recalled. "After he received us he had some of his civilized Indians come with their wagons to take us up to Fort Simcoe. They did not come because they loved us, or because they were Christians. No; they were just like all

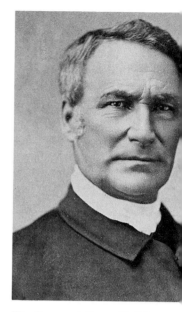

The Reverend James H. Wilbur, Indian agent for the Yakima Reservation in Washington Territory, had no sympathy for the hungry, shivering Paiutes. To dramatize their wretched plight, Winnemucca led a parade of naked Paiutes into one of Wilbur's Yakima prayer meetings, but not even that awoke the stony clergyman's sympathy.

civilized people; they came . . . because they were to be paid for it."

Winnemucca's resentment of Wilbur and the Yakima Indians only grew stronger in the months that followed. The Paiutes were poorly housed and fed, and many of them died before the spring came. To make matters worse, the Yakimas disliked the strangers from the south and commandeered most of the Paiutes' horses. Winnemucca begged Wilbur to intercede, but he was unwilling to help. And to add to Winnemucca's burdens, her beloved sister-in-law Mattie died on May 29, 1879, from injuries she had sustained while falling from a horse.

When Winnemucca at last received some pay for her work with the army during the Bannock war, she decided to take action. She traveled north to Vancouver Barracks, where General Howard was stationed, and told him of her intention to go to Washington, D.C., to urge the BIA to release her people from Yakima. Howard was sympathetic to her plea and gave her letters of recommendation to government officials he knew in the nation's capital.

Next, Winnemucca took a steamer to San Francisco, met with Natchez, and began a campaign to garner publicity for the plight of her tribe. She lectured, quite successfully, through November and early December. With the proceeds from her talks, Winnemucca returned with Natchez to his home in Lovelock, Nevada, and prepared for her important journey east.

7

IN THE PUBLIC FORUM

In late 1879, while Sarah Winnemucca was in Lovelock, Nevada, with her brother Natchez, a letter arrived from the BIA, inviting her to Washington, D.C., to speak with Secretary of the Interior Carl Schurz. At last, Winnemucca was being taken seriously by a high government official. Before she set out for the nation's capital, however, she prepared to meet with a man named Hayworth, the official who had sent her the invitation; he was coming to Nevada, he said, to inquire into the Paiutes' unrest.

The BIA was well aware of the Paiutes' unhappy situation. Winnemucca's lectures had attracted a great deal of attention, and during her talks she never hesitated to name the agents she felt had wronged the Paiutes; the BIA said it was troubled by her accusations. Moreover, the situation at Malheur Reservation had become impossible to ignore. During the past year, not a single Paiute had consented to live at Malheur, thus putting W. V. Rinehart in a difficult spot.

When Hayworth arrived in Nevada and met with Winnemucca, he quickly persuaded her, Natchez, and Old Winnemucca to travel with him to Washington, D.C. He convinced Winnemucca that their trip would proceed more easily if he acted as their escort. But the main reason that the BIA representative wanted to accompany the three Paiutes was that he had no intention of letting them

Joined by Captain Jim of the Paiutes (second from right) and an unidentified white boy, the Winnemuccas (left to right: Sarah, Old Winnemucca, Natchez) gather for a portrait in 1880. Shortly afterward, the three Winnemuccas headed for Washington, D.C., to meet with Secretary of the Interior Carl Schurz.

93

go anywhere or do anything that would generate publicity for the Paiutes.

The small group left Nevada on January 13, 1880. Mindful of making a good impression, Winnemucca wore a smart outfit comparable to what well-dressed non-Indian women of the era wore. Old Winnemucca had on his customary garb, a somewhat modified version of military dress put together from various donations from friendly U.S. Army officers.

The party arrived in Washington, D.C., one week later. Hayworth hustled the Paiutes into a hotel and accompanied them everywhere they went in an itinerary that included a great amount of sightseeing. The BIA representative had no intention of letting Winnemucca lecture in public or give interviews to reporters. As soon as she realized that Hayworth was trying to keep her quiet, Winnemucca understood that her accusations could prove extremely embarrassing to the U.S. government.

Before a lecture could be set up, the Paiutes were ushered into the office of the secretary of the interior. Upon hearing their sad story, Schurz seemed surprisingly sympathetic and raised Winnemucca's hopes by giving her a promising letter. It stated that the Paiutes should be allowed to live at Malheur, with every head of a family and single adult male being given an allotment of 160 acres of land. The letter also said that the Paiutes who were being held at Yakima would be allowed to return to Malheur—at their own expense—and that all Paiutes employed outside the reservation would not be forced to live on the reservation as long as they could support themselves.

A few days later, after more sightseeing, Winnemucca contacted a newspaper reporter to help her arrange a public lecture. Getting wind of what she was up to, Hayworth informed Schurz of Winnemucca's plan, then called her into his office. There Hayworth said that as

For Winnemucca, the nation's capital (pictured in the 1880s) seemed full of good news: The powerful and apparently sympathetic Secretary Schurz promised to give the Paiutes freedom to travel, freedom to choose their place of residence, free land, even free canvas for tents. "He told me [the government] would grant all I asked of them for my people," Winnemucca recalled.

the recipient of aid from the BIA she should not criticize the government. Hayworth's veiled threat prompted Winnemucca to cancel the upcoming public lecture.

The next day, she took part in a much more private gathering. Winnemucca, Natchez, and Old Winnemucca attended a reception where they were introduced to President Hayes and his wife. The meeting consisted of little more than a handshake, for Hayworth was still careful to prevent Winnemucca from speaking out. Even so, she relished coming face-to-face with the president. He did not seem to "be made of wood or rock," she said, and hoped that was a sign all would be well.

After the reception, Winnemucca exacted a promise from Schurz to send 100 tents to Lovelock, Nevada. She planned to distribute the tents to the Paiutes when they gathered to hear the results of her trip to the nation's capital. Then Winnemucca, Natchez, and Old Winnemucca set out for Nevada.

When the trio reached Lovelock, a large number of Paiutes was already present to hear the outcome of the journey. They gathered in the winter cold, without adequate shelter, and waited in vain for the arrival of the tents and supplies Schurz had promised. "While we were waiting we almost starved," Winnemucca remembered. "I wrote to the Secretary of the Interior for God's sake to send us something to eat. He answered my letter telling me to take my people to the Malheur Agency. Just think of my taking my people, who were already starving, to go three hundred miles through snow waist-deep." After she read them Schurz's reply, one Paiute stood up to speak, noting that the non-Indians must be very forgetful, for they often promised what they did not do.

In any event, the Paiutes scattered, convinced that the Winnemuccas' expedition had done no good. Old Winnemucca returned to his band, Natchez resettled at Lovelock, and Sarah labored to prove that their work had not been in vain. The letter from Schurz continued to serve as the centerpiece of her faith that the Paiutes would receive what they had been promised. She traveled about the area, visiting different bands of Paiutes and begging them to go to Malheur to receive their land. When the Paiutes told her they would go to Malheur only if Leggins's band at Yakima could also return, she decided to visit Yakima and present Father Wilbur with Schurz's letter.

After making the long trip north, Winnemucca told Wilbur of her visit to Washington, D.C. He reacted with anger and adamantly opposed the release of the Paiutes, pointing out that he had received no letter confirming the one Schurz had given her. He immediately wrote to Washington, D.C., branding Winnemucca a troublemaker intent on disturbing the Paiutes in his care for her own benefit. She was unaware that Rinehart had also mailed out claims from some of his employees that she was

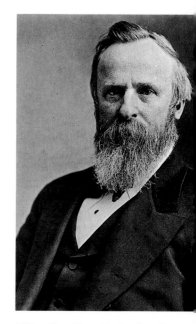

When President Rutherford B. Hayes met Winnemucca during her 1880 visit to Washington, D.C., he shook her hand and asked, "Did you get all you want for your people?" She replied, "Yes, sir, as far as I know"—but time would prove her sadly mistaken. Schurz's sweeping promises, she said later, "like the wind, were heard no more."

undependable and worthless as a representative of the Paiutes. In government circles, suspicion of Winnemucca's motives grew.

Wilbur still felt threatened by Winnemucca, however, and he offered her money to keep the contents of Schurz's letter secret from Leggins's band. He also attempted to bribe her by hiring her as an interpreter. Winnemucca turned aside Wilbur's underhanded efforts and read Schurz's letter to the Paiutes. In July, she wrote to Natchez that she was preparing to bring Leggins's band south.

As the Paiutes readied themselves for the long journey, Wilbur claimed that the Indians could not travel such a distance alone. They would require a military escort to prevent non-Indians from killing them along the way. He then delayed in assembling his troops, until he finally received the telegram he had been waiting for: Schurz's message said that the best course would be for the Paiutes to remain at Yakima because it was too dangerous for them to travel.

With no one to turn to except for General Howard, Winnemucca journeyed to Vancouver Barracks. Although he was unable to do anything for the Paiutes in Yakima, he gave Winnemucca a job teaching and interpreting for Bannock prisoners. Meanwhile, Wilbur continued his campaign against releasing the Paiutes. On October 31, 1880, he received a letter from the BIA announcing that Malheur had been officially abandoned as a reservation for the Paiutes. They were destined to remain at Yakima.

Winnemucca's only consolation from the U.S. government was that the army finally paid her for her work during the Bannock war. She received $500, which she saved carefully.

Another personally rewarding event soon took place. While accompanying some Bannocks being sent to Fort Hall, Winnemucca passed through Idaho, and at Henry's

Lake she met her sister Elma. They had not seen each other in years. Elma was living with her husband, John Smith, and the two sisters had a joyful reunion. Excited to be in touch with her family once again, Elma traveled with Sarah to the town of Winnemucca, where they visited relatives, then proceeded to see Natchez and his family at Lovelock.

Eventually, Winnemucca headed for San Francisco, where she married for the third time; on December 5, 1881, she wed Virginian Lewis H. Hopkins. The newlyweds stayed in San Francisco for several weeks, as Winnemucca planned for a lecture tour of the East. Despite the personal concerns that had occupied her over the past few months, she was still determined to help the Paiutes being held at Yakima. In addition, she and her family had lost much of the esteem of the tribe after their unproductive visit with Schurz, and Winnemucca wanted to regain her good name.

The trip, however, never came off as planned. Apparently, Hopkins gambled away his wife's carefully

Paiute women gather pine nuts near Lovelock, the Nevada community where Natchez and a group of other tribe members had settled. As time passed, bringing ever-increasing numbers of non-Indians to take possession of former hunting and foraging grounds, the Paiutes' traditional methods of survival became harder and harder to maintain.

guarded $500. So, instead of heading east, the couple stayed with Winnemucca's brother Tom at Pyramid Lake, then settled in Idaho with Elma in February 1882.

That summer, the Paiutes' woes mounted. First, the land on which Malheur Reservation was located was sold at a public auction. Next, in July, Leggins prepared to lead 43 families on a daring escape, but they were discovered and forced back to Yakima. That same month, Old Winnemucca, who was more than 90 years old, married a widow with a young child. After the wedding, he embarked on a journey to meet with another chief but fell ill outside Coppersmith Ranch, Nevada. He died three months later, on October 21, 1881.

Throughout 1881, Winnemucca saved money and prepared to go east with her husband. In the meantime, she wrote a long article about Indians that appeared in *The Californian* and saw the letter she had written to Major Douglass 12 years earlier get reprinted in *A Century of Dishonor*, a history of the government's mistreatment of Indians by the popular writer Helen Hunt Jackson. Winnemucca did not return to the East Coast until 1883. When she did, she was warmly received. A number of people were taking a growing interest in Indian affairs.

Two sisters from a prominent New England family, Mary Peabody Mann and Elizabeth Palmer Peabody, emerged as Winnemucca's most ardent supporters. Mary was the widow of educator Horace Mann, who helped develop public education in the United States. Elizabeth was a noted lecturer and writer on a variety of historical topics and published the writings of such philosophers as Henry David Thoreau and Ralph Waldo Emerson. Their sister Sophie, who died at a young age, had been married to the novelist Nathaniel Hawthorne.

Elizabeth Peabody apparently suggested to Winnemucca that she give a series of lectures, to be paid for by subscription, rather than hold individual lectures, as she had done in San Francisco. Winnemucca agreed, ultimately embarking on a successful series of speaking engagements throughout New England and New York. She was particularly in demand to speak before church groups and Indian Associations (groups of women interested in privately aiding Indian tribes). In her lectures, she forcefully reminded her audiences that Indians were not U.S. citizens and enjoyed none of the advantages of citizenship.

Winnemucca did not hold back. She asserted that the Paiutes had become impoverished because of corrupt BIA agents, and she mentioned the specific agents she had found to be greedy, cruel, and unsympathetic. She also said that the Paiutes' experiences with the U.S. Army had been agreeable, and she commended the army officers with whom she had dealt.

The BIA officials became extremely upset by her claims and suspicious of her praise for the army, and they did not hesitate to strike back. In *The Council Fire and Arbitrator*, a periodical strongly supported by the bureau, one writer characterized Winnemucca as "an Amazonian champion of the Army [who] was being used as a tool of the Army officers to create public sentiment in favor of the transfer of the Indian Bureau to the War Department." The department publicized the affidavits sent by Rinehart to discredit Winnemucca and assailed her honesty, motives, and morals.

The BIA's attack on her character deeply upset Winnemucca. Accordingly, she embraced the idea when Peabody and Mann urged her to write an autobiography. Not only would such a book make money for the Paiute cause, it would also provide information about Winnemucca for those who did not know much about her past. In the Paiute way of life, the best answer to enemies and critics was a proud recounting of deeds and actions,

Lewis H. Hopkins, Winnemucca's third husband, turned out to be as poor a choice as his predecessors. A habitual gambler and a spendthrift, Hopkins also passed bad checks, many of them to Winnemucca's friends. "So long as she is his wife," remarked one disapproving acquaintance, "he will rob her of all the money she earns." The prediction would prove all too accurate.

and that is exactly what Winnemucca sat down to do in writing her autobiography.

Originally published in 1883, *Life Among the Piutes* remains a unique document because it was the first published book written entirely by an Indian woman. Nevertheless, Winnemucca was already following an established tradition in recounting her life for the public. In *American Indian Autobiography*, author H. David Brumble points out that "Indians of many tribes were answering their accusers with autobiographical narratives long before the Paiutes came into contact with the white man." Brumble also notes: "In many ways, *Life Among the Piutes* assumes an audience with Paiute habits of mind. . . . [Winnemucca] is what she has accomplished . . . she is the sum of her reputation."

Despite its precedents in Indian culture, *Life Among the Piutes* was quite an undertaking. Mary Mann, who edited Winnemucca's writing, noted that "spelling is an unknown quantity to her" and labored over the spelling and grammar of the book. Yet the words and form of the autobiography remain entirely Winnemucca's own.

Winnemucca worked on the book in Boston, where she stayed with the Peabody sisters when not traveling to lectures. Hopkins accompanied her everywhere and proved helpful, for he introduced her to audiences and did research for her book at the Boston Atheneum and the Library of Congress in Washington, D.C. Whereas Mann edited what Winnemucca wrote, Peabody enthusiastically raised money to pay for the publication of *Life Among the Piutes*. Among those who contributed to the $600 needed to publish the book were the poet John Greenleaf Whittier and Mrs. Ralph Waldo Emerson, in whose homes Winnemucca lectured.

When published, *Life Among the Piutes* was 268 pages long, with the title stamped in gold on the cover. The book also contained a 20-page appendix of letters attesting

New Englander Mary Peabody Mann, a fervent supporter of education, wholeheartedly admired Winnemucca and her pioneering schools for Indian children. Mann both inspired Winnemucca to write her 1883 book, Life Among the Piutes: Their Wrongs and Claims, *and edited the final work, which she called a "heroic act on the part of the writer."*

to Winnemucca's truthfulness and character. A subscription for 10 copies of the book cost $1. Winnemucca also sold signed copies for buyers after her lectures.

Throughout 1883, Winnemucca lectured in Providence, Rhode Island; Hartford, Connecticut; New York City, Newburgh, and Poughkeepsie, New York (where she appeared at Vassar College); Dorset, Vermont; and Boston, Salem, Cambridge, Germantown, and Pittsfield, Massachusetts. Early in 1884, she and Hopkins moved to Baltimore, Maryland, and she continued to lecture in the area.

As Winnemucca's fame grew, she was invited to the home of Senator Henry L. Dawes, who was chairman of the U.S. Senate subcommittee that dealt with Indian affairs. Greatly impressed by the 39-year-old Winnemucca, Dawes promised to call her before the committee to testify at its next session. Meanwhile, she circulated a petition seeking citizenship for Indians and eventually gathered a total of 5,000 signatures.

Winnemucca's petition was presented to Congress and sent to the Senate subcommittee on Indian affairs during the first session of 1884. Soon afterward, she was called to appear before Dawes's subcommittee. She answered his questions about the Paiutes and stated her case. In particular, she proposed that a reservation for the Paiutes be established at the underutilized Camp McDermit to replace the vanished Malheur Agency. She also asked that all the heads of family be allotted land of their own and that the money and goods granted by Congress to the Paiutes be administered by the U.S. Army and not the BIA or its agents.

Winnemucca's hopes rose and fell through the spring as congressional bills were written, amended, and passed or referred to different committees. In the House of Representatives, a bill granting McDermit to the Paiutes eventually passed, to Winnemucca's great joy. But when members of the Department of War argued that it still needed the fort at McDermit, the Senate refused to pass the bill as it currently stood.

As the jockeying for an approved bill continued, Winnemucca learned that Leggins's band had finally freed itself from Yakima. These Paiutes had successfully escaped after Wilbur retired, and his replacement, R. H. Milroy, did not coerce them into returning. He evidently realized that they had been miserable at Yakima, and when he discovered that they had returned to their homeland, he recommended to his superiors they be allowed to remain there.

More news arrived on July 6, 1884, when the Senate approved its version of the bill that dealt directly with Paiute affairs. The senators voted to allow Leggins's band and what remained of Old Winnemucca's band to return to Pyramid Lake, where each head of a family would receive 160 acres, to be administered by the secretary of the interior. Winnemucca could not help but think the bill was a bitter defeat. It affirmed the BIA's control of the Paiutes and condemned them to Pyramid Lake, where squatters had taken all the good land years before. Although the bill appeared to provide for Leggins's people—destitute after fleeing Yakima—there was neither land nor any means of sustenance for them at Pyramid Lake.

More bad news followed. Hopkins became ill, probably with tuberculosis, and Winnemucca was informed by her bank that he had been drawing large checks from her account, apparently to cover gambling debts and to help out his friends and acquaintances. When Hopkins learned that his wife had discovered his activities, he abandoned her and left town in spite of his poor health. By then, Winnemucca had only a few hundred dollars left from all the money she had raised. Bitterly disappointed, she returned west and stayed with Elma, writing to Peabody and Mann that all was lost. She could no longer help her people.

After getting in touch with BIA officials, Peabody and Mann advised Winnemucca to go to Pyramid Lake to see if she could do anything there. Winnemucca agreed; on the way, she saw Natchez and paid a debt he owed, so she arrived at Pyramid Lake with only $50. McMaster, the agent, did not want any new Paiute bands at what he regarded as his reservation, and most of the Paiutes in the McDermit area did not want to go to Pyramid Lake. A weary round of visits to McMaster, his replacement, and the Paiutes ensued for Winnemucca. She had nowhere to stay and lived in an unheated karnee.

As the winter approached, Winnemucca came down with terrible chills and fever. By the end of the year, she realized she was not doing any good. The Paiutes did not want to go to Pyramid Lake, and the agents did not want

Elizabeth Palmer Peabody, Mary Mann's sister and an equally devoted friend to Winnemucca, was a classic New England bluestocking—an energetic, intellectual, literary-minded woman. Born in 1804, she lived 90 years, during which she worked as a teacher, ran a bookshop, published elementary textbooks, opened the first American kindergarten, published an educational magazine, and wrote several biographies.

them there. Furthermore, the Paiutes mistrusted her because her trip east had proved fruitless.

Still, Winnemucca would not give up. She decided to take an entirely different approach. Perhaps if the Paiutes could devise a plan for living entirely apart from the reservation system and the BIA, the government might see fit to help them thrive. Encouraged by Peabody and Mann, she decided to make Natchez's farm a model system of living for the Paiutes, where they could work communally at farming, and where she could teach school and help them. With a new idea and renewed determination, Winnemucca prepared to face the upcoming year.

8

▼～▼～▼

LOOKING TO THE NEXT GENERATION

Booked for another series of lectures, Winnemucca traveled to San Francisco in early 1885. By then, she had already written to Elizabeth Peabody and Mary Mann about her idea for Natchez's farm, and they had responded positively. The two women, in fact, had not only supported the plan, but also promised to raise money for it from eastern philanthropists. Winnemucca, of course, intended to do her part as well. Her lectures in San Francisco were well attended, and she saved the money they brought in for her project.

Winnemucca's trip east, especially her stay in Washington, had given her a more sophisticated approach to the Indian's position in the United States. Now she began to compare the government's treatment of Native Americans with its treatment of the Europeans who were crowding into the cities during the great immigration wave of the 1880s. She told her San Francisco audiences that she wished she could put "all the Indians of Nevada on ships in our harbor, take them to New York and land them there as immigrants, that they might be received with open arms, blessed with the blessings of universal suffrage [voting rights] and thus placed beyond the

The San Francisco Call *ran this picture of 41-year-old Winnemucca during her 1885 lecture series. "Her apparel was of dressed deerskin, buff-colored and heavily fringed with beads," said the newspaper caption. "Pendant at her side was a handsomely embroidered pouch. Her black hair, which reached below her waist, was brushed smoothly back from her forehead."*

107

necessity of reservation help and out of the reach of Indian agents."

During Winnemucca's lecture tour, Natchez came to visit her. On several occasions, he appeared onstage with her, and at the end of the tour, he accompanied her back to Lovelock. There, Winnemucca set about opening an Indian-run school and Natchez prepared to turn his farmland into a communal enterprise—something many agents had promised but failed to do with Paiute reservation land.

In May, learning that her brother Tom was gravely ill at Pyramid Lake, Winnemucca raced to his bedside. Just before he died, Tom thanked her for her help throughout his life, and told her he was leaving her his farm. Winnemucca, close to all her siblings, was deeply grieved, but anger mixed with her sorrow when she observed the rough coffin and cheap funeral allotted to Tom by Mr. Gibson, the Pyramid Lake agent. In the *Daily Silver State* she wrote of her disgust with Gibson's contemptuous treatment of the Paiutes. The article however, also contained an upbeat note: In it, she announced the opening of her Paiute school at Lovelock.

That summer she taught 26 Paiute children, many of whom spoke no English. Winnemucca, who was fluent in Paiute, English, and several other Indian dialects, proved herself a gifted and resourceful teacher. To teach the children English, she began by asking them to say a Paiute word, which she then repeated in English and spelled out on the blackboard. Next, she instructed them to copy the English spelling and say the word aloud in English. Canfield notes that by the end of the summer, the students were chalking English words on fenceposts around the farm. Winnemucca also taught the students arithmetic and drawing, all the while keeping them mindful of their Paiute history and heritage.

Pleased with the first results of her teaching, Winnemucca sent examples of the children's work to Peabody and Mann, who used it to raise further money for the school. Winnemucca was so enthusiastic that she worked all day and sometimes most of the night. The pace began to take its toll: She experienced increasing bouts of chills and fever. She was also suffering from arthritis, a painful, chronic condition that had started bothering her two years earlier and that was growing worse.

Winter was coming, and Winnemucca, if she were not to become a serious invalid, would need a warm, secure residence. Aware of this necessity, Peabody and Mann sent goods and money for the construction of a solid house in which Winnemucca could both teach and live. The two New Englanders also tried to find an experienced teacher to help Winnemucca in the classroom, but here they failed; Winnemucca continued to teach alone and to complete the house on her own.

Meanwhile, Natchez was having his own problems, particularly in gaining access to water for his crops. His white neighbors resented the presence of an Indian farmer—especially one who dared consider himself their equal—and they made it their business to obstruct his plans for expansion and to keep him away from community water sources. To make matters worse, some of the area's landowners trespassed on his land and made use of his own meager water supplies.

In December, Winnemucca finally finished building her combined home and schoolhouse. The following February, a group of Lovelock citizens came to visit the school and observe the children. Afterward, their spokeswoman wrote to Peabody and Mann, commending the students' progress and marveling over their newfound ability to name objects in English, recite the days of the week and months of the year, calculate four-figure

numbers, and spell their own name aloud. Particularly impressive to the self-appointed committee was the class's singing of gospel hymns in perfect time.

Peabody and Mann continued to aid the projects developed by Winnemucca and her brother. When Natchez, for example, realized that his neighbors were stealing his water rights and grazing their cattle on his land, he told the New England women about it. They sent him money to hire a surveyor and to put up fences. Soon after that, Winnemucca decided that the children, instead of joining the tribe's pine-nut expedition each spring, would benefit by staying at the school year-round; Mann and Peabody obligingly arranged a $100 monthly payment for the students' board.

Soon after she got the school under way, Winnemucca learned that railroad baron Leland Stanford, who had recently been elected U.S. senator from California, was expected to visit the area soon. Stanford, the man who had given Natchez his farm years earlier, was recognized for his generosity to education; among his projects, for example, was the California institution known today as Stanford University.

Winnemucca and Natchez knew that Stanford could greatly help their people. If he was impressed with the Peabody Indian School (as Winnemucca had named her

A group of Lovelock Paiutes harvest wheat in 1897. Natchez, who used similar traditional methods on his Lovelock farm, turned the acreage into a communal project, where workers shared both labor and profits. Natchez's farm also served as an outdoor classroom for Winnemucca's students.

venture) and with Natchez's farm, he might agree to support other enterprises that were operated not only for Indians but *by* Indians, rather than operated for Indians by federal agents and reservation officials. Excited by the prospect of Stanford's visit, brother and sister set about putting school and farm in the best possible order.

Winnemucca daydreamed that, after seeing her school, Stanford would return to Washington and demand that the BIA fund many more such schools. She did not know when—or even if—Stanford would visit, but she was happy that, thanks to Peabody and Mann, her children would be present whenever a visitor appeared.

The Peabody Indian School unquestionably needed more help. For one thing, although the student body had increased in size and the children were happy and making good progress, the school had no official existence. The U.S. government recognized only two boarding schools for Indians: the Hampton Institute in Virginia and Carlisle Indian School in Pennsylvania.

Both Hampton and Carlisle were run by non-Indians, and both espoused a teaching philosophy entirely unlike Winnemucca's. They promoted total immersion in non-Indian culture, taught no Indian history, and forbade students to speak their own languages or wear their own clothing. The schools discouraged correspondence between the children and their parents, and they punished students for displaying any "Indian" behavior. Harsh as they were, these rules were probably well meant; the directors felt that the children would be more successful in the non-Indian world if they were as non-Indian as possible.

Winnemucca was well aware of the problems facing Indians in a non-Indian culture—she had, after all, spent most of her life trying to bridge the two worlds and retain her own personality at the same time. She seemed to draw strength from her Indian heritage, and she was uncompromisingly proud of her Paiute identity. She also realized that the Paiutes could not isolate themselves, and she strove to help them and herself make their way among non-Indians. Her school and her educational philosophy were based on her own experience—something the founders of the Carlisle and Hampton institutes could never claim.

Nevertheless, Winnemucca made no headway in gaining the government's backing, and it soon became clear that she probably never would. In 1886, an federal official visited the Peabody Indian School and informed Winnemucca that neither school nor farm would receive a penny of government funding unless she gave up the school directorship and Natchez gave up ownership of his land. Non-Indians would not support the enterprise unless they ran it. Deeply insulted, Winnemucca and Natchez refused even to consider abandoning their cherished projects.

Several months later, Winnemucca got an assistant at last: Arriving in Lovelock in August 1886 was Alice Chapin, a young easterner whose interest in the Paiutes had been sparked by Peabody and Mann. Delighted with Chapin's presence, Winnemucca also appreciated her gift: a supply of quinine, the malaria medication that eases the type of chills and fever Winnemucca had long endured. She and Chapin liked and respected one another and were soon energetically working side by side. They devoted mornings to classroom subjects and afternoons to such practical matters as cooking, sewing, and (under Natchez's supervision) farm work.

Natchez did what he could to help the two teachers, but he already had his hands full, trying to farm while dealing with the hostility of his non-Indian neighbors. Typical of his problems was the trouble he experienced with the local water company. The company's workers had entered Natchez's property without his permission,

An unknown local artist drew this portrait of Natchez, who, like his sister, usually wore settler-style clothing in public. Despite the concentrated opposition of his bigoted neighbors, Natchez worked his Lovelock farm profitably until 1886, when resentful local farmers goaded his workers into a revolt that finally drove him off the land.

tapped his streams and wells, and dug irrigation ditches that carried his precious water not only to his own fields but to his white neighbors' farms as well.

Adding insult to injury, the company then ordered Natchez to do most of the maintenance on the ditches and to leave his gates open to allow them access. The neighbors' cattle happily wandered through the open gates to graze in Natchez's grain fields.

Understandably worried about his carefully tended crops, Natchez engaged an old Paiute man to watch the gates and shoo away the cows. Soon after that, the company cut off Natchez's water supply, claiming that he and his Paiute workers had failed to do their share in maintaining the irrigation ditches. When Natchez complained to local authorities, the water company manager hotly defended his operation's move, saying the Paiutes were irresponsible and too lazy to work. To prove his point, he gave an example: an old man who, he said, did nothing but sit by the gates all day.

Natchez eventually forced the company to turn his water back on, but both farm and school still faced serious difficulties. To begin with, after all the Paiutes' hopes and dreams, Stanford never showed up. Then Natchez ran into major trouble with his Paiute farmhands. He had earlier proposed, and they had agreed, that he would pay them for their summer of work in grain rather than cash. That way, they could wait until the market price rose, then sell the grain at a good profit.

Right after the September harvest of 1886, Natchez was preparing to distribute the workers' shares of grain when they suddenly demanded to be paid in cash instead of crops. Natchez was appalled; he did not have that amount of cash on hand, and he did not understand why his people had changed their minds. At that point, he could not know that the local non-Indian farmers, determined to see him fail, had been spreading malicious rumors. Elizabeth Peabody had been sending Winnemucca money each month to help support her boarding students; the farmers told Natchez's workers that easterners were sending the tribe $100 per month, but that Natchez and Winnemucca were keeping it for themselves.

Winnemucca realized that by this time, tempers had grown so hot that the only recourse was to get some money somehow and give it to the angry workers. Turning to the only source she knew, she fired off a frantic telegram to Peabody and Mann, asking them to send her $200 at once. The New England women found the wire puzzling; it said nothing about what was happening or about why the money was needed. They decided to wait for a further explanation before sending anything. The decision almost doomed the farm and school.

Natchez had to pay the Paiutes as soon as possible. To raise the cash, he immediately sold all the harvested grain—at a price far lower than it would have brought if sold later. Now, no profits were left to support the farm and school for the next year. Natchez left his land and went to work as a cowhand, just as he had done as a boy in California.

Winnemucca took a job as a housekeeper, then wrote a despairing letter to Peabody about the situation. Peabody responded with an encouraging letter: She had ordered the printing of 200 more copies of *Life Among the Piutes*, the proceeds from which would help finance the farm and school during the next year. She also informed Winnemucca that she had written and published a short pamphlet, *Sarah Winnemucca's Practical Solution to the Indian Problem*, which would be sold to assist the Paiutes.

In November, Winnemucca managed to return to the farm and reopen the school. Delighted by this turn of events, the Paiutes sent her 45 children. Some of them

Students line up for inspection at the federally run Indian school in Grand Junction, Colorado. Winnemucca successfully fought a government effort to remove her Paiute students to Grand Junction in 1887, but she was never able to obtain federal funds for her own school, which closed in 1888.

even came from Pyramid Lake; they much preferred Winnemucca's school to the one operated by reservation agent Gibson, even though his was federally supported and far better equipped. The Peabody Indian School functioned smoothly through much of the winter, but bad news arrived in February 1887.

First, Winnemucca learned that Mary Mann had died. Although she left her small savings to Winnemucca, the money could not replace the quiet strength and encouragement of one of Winnemucca's staunchest patrons. The next blow was the passage of the General Allotment Act (also known as the Dawes Act). This federal legislation, steered through Congress by Senator Dawes, terminated the status of tribes as "domestic nations." Under the act, which was designed to end the reservation system, each Indian head of family would receive 160 acres of land in trust. After 25 years, the Indians would receive both full title to the acreage and American citizenship. No agents would dispense goods or tell the Indians what to plant or what they could earn.

The Paiutes had never flourished under the reservation system, and Winnemucca supported the Dawes Act. She could not know that it would prove worse than the system it replaced; eventually leading to the weakening of tribal and communal ties, it would also result in non-Indian speculators' obtaining most of the best Indian land. These ill effects would take time to show themselves, but the act also caused Winnemucca immediate distress.

Winnemucca had this mourning card printed for her husband in 1887. To the exasperation of friends and relatives, she had never lost her affectionate trust in Lewis Hopkins, despite his almost constant misbehavior.

The Dawes Act was intended to speed the Indians' assimilation into the non-Indian mainstream. To accomplish that goal, it mandated that all Indian children be educated in government-run schools where only English was spoken. Within months of the act's passage, a federal official visited the Peabody Indian School and told Winnemucca to prepare her pupils for a journey. In accordance with the new law, he explained, he was going to take the Indian children to a new government boarding school in Grand Junction, Colorado.

Winnemucca flatly refused. At this point in the year, many of the students' parents were off hunting or gathering pine nuts, and Winnemucca would allow no one to take the children without their parents' approval. Her students remained at Lovelock. The government, however, did remove 12 Paiute children from Pyramid Lake, including one son of Winnemucca's half brother Lee, who was on a visit to San Francisco at the time.

Calling on the last of her resources, Winnemucca decided to turn her operation into a trade school where Indian children could learn job-related skills. The school she envisioned would not compete directly with the government boarding schools, and the students would be able to remain near their relatives and friends, an extremely important consideration to Paiutes. Having made up her mind, she once again traveled east, this time to raise money for the proposed trade school.

This visit proved to be her least productive, for several reasons. The general public felt that the Dawes Act had solved "the Indian problem." The Indian associations that had once clamored to hear Winnemucca speak were now focusing on the schools created by the act. Even Peabody, who had long shared many of Winnemucca's teaching ideals, had gone on to other interests.

For Winnemucca, the brightest spot on this trip was an unexpected encounter with her long-absent husband,

Lewis Hopkins. Perhaps she needed someone to raise her flagging spirits, someone to offer comfort about her failure to gain support for her school; whatever the reason, she agreed to a reconciliation with Hopkins, and when she returned to Lovelock in the fall, he went with her.

Hopkins's reappearance pleased almost no one. Natchez could not abide him. Peabody and her friends, some of them still holding bad checks from Hopkins, disapproved as well. "So long as she [Winnemucca] is his wife," commented one acquaintance dourly, "he will rob her of all the money she earns." Natchez claimed that Hopkins did little on the farm but eat, sleep, cough, and refuse to work.

More energetic at harvest time, Hopkins transported Natchez's 400 sacks of grain to the town of Winnemucca and sold them. When he returned to Loveland, however, he rekindled his brother-in-law's anger by offering him only a small share of the proceeds. Winnemucca failed to object to her husband's high-handed behavior, which made Natchez more resentful still. Hopkins then took the money and headed for San Francisco, where he spent at least part of it on doctors—again, with Winnemucca's apparent approval.

Hopkins eventually returned to Lovelock, but by then his health was ruined; he died of tuberculosis in October 1887. His list of misdeeds had been long: He had abused his wife's trust, abandoned her, caused a sharp rift between her and her brother, and collapsed her dreams of a trade school by taking the harvest money. Nevertheless, Winnemucca now behaved as a loving widow, observing the customary rituals of mourning and even ordering a memorial card printed.

Not long after her husband's death, Winnemucca started running a small day school, which she operated through the following winter. In the spring of 1888, she learned that the Interior Department had taken posses-

Elma Winnemucca Smith relaxes outside her home in Henry's Lake, Montana, in 1919. She died in 1920, outliving her beloved younger sister Sarah by 29 years.

sion of Fort McDermit and was planning to turn it over to the Paiutes at last. An optimistic and ambitious 18-year-old Winnemucca might have rejoiced over this news; a tired, resigned 44-year-old Winnemucca found it of little interest.

When summer came and her students departed on the pine-nut expeditions, Winnemucca took stock. The government would not support her teaching efforts in any way. The Dawes Act had effectively dried up the springs of private philanthropy for Indians. The proceeds from Natchez's farm alone could not support the Peabody Indian School. The whole enterprise of the combined farm and school, run by and for Paiutes, had received not even a hint of official recognition, commendation, or assistance. Winnemucca had dreamed of a Paiute nation that could deal with the white world and yet maintain its own identity, but the dream had proved no match for reality or "progress." Winnemucca's great experiment, in short, was over.

Historical records show that Winnemucca closed her school permanently in the summer of 1888, but little is known of her specific activities after that. In September 1889, a local newspaper reported that she and Natchez attended an Indian gathering at Elko, Nevada. From that point on, she apparently spent part of her time in Lovelock with Natchez and part at Henry's Lake, Montana, with their sister Elma, who had adopted two orphaned non-Indian boys.

Elma's husband died in January 1889, but she kept her house and land, and her sons took good care of her. Local residents later recalled the two Indian sisters walking around Henry's Lake in 1890, chatting with their young neighbors and gathering plants and berries. Winnemucca was only 46 years old in 1890, but her health, always fragile, was now deteriorating rapidly. Her arthritis had gotten worse, her bouts of chills and fever were increasing.

In the fall of 1891, she went to visit Elma at Henry's Lake; on October 17, 1891, she died there peacefully.

Winnemucca had spent her life in both the Indian and non-Indian worlds, and her death was news in both. The Bannock Indians in the area gathered to give her a traditional Indian burial, attended by Natchez and her other relatives. The headline of her *New York Times* obituary, appearing on the newspaper's first page on October 27, read: PRINCESS WINNEMUCCA DEAD: THE MOST REMARKABLE WOMAN AMONG THE PIUTES OF NEVADA.

The *Times* story mentioned Winnemucca's marriages to Bartlett and to Hopkins, whom it called "a well-educated, handsome young man and an inveterate gambler" who "spent all the money she made." Providing a long list of Winnemucca's accomplishments, the article also mentioned the exploits of her grandfather Captain Truckee, her education, her lecture tours "under the auspices of Miss Elizabeth Peabody," her autobiography,

Paiute youngsters assemble at a Nevada Indian school in the early 1900s. For many decades, such schools deliberately suppressed Indian language and culture, but by the mid-20th century, the tide was turning: Indians began to rediscover their identity and to insist that their children learn about and take pride in their heritage. Sarah Winnemucca, who worked so hard for the right to educate Indian children in Indian ways, would surely have been pleased by that.

her school at Lovelock, and her employment by General Howard during the Bannock War. In his book *Famous Indian Chiefs I Have Known*, Howard wrote:

> She did our government great service, and if I could tell you but a tenth part of all she willingly did to help the white settlers and her own people to live peaceably together I am sure you would think, as I do, that the name of Toc-me-to-ne [Shellflower] should have a place beside the name of Pocahontas in the history of our country.

Sarah Winnemucca undeniably helped her people, but she was unable to establish the educational system she considered essential to the Paiutes' longterm well-being. In the 19th century, her ideas about her people's values struck many Americans as out of step with the times. Today, almost a century and a half after her birth, those ideas are voiced more and more frequently.

Winnemucca's approach to education is increasingly followed by modern Native Americans, who also proudly embrace their Indian identity. Just as Winnemucca did, these 20th-century Indians are struggling to maintain their heritage in a non-Indian world. In *Life Among the Piutes*, Winnemucca tried to tell non-Indians about the Paiutes and their place in the history of the United States; more than a century later, Indians are still trying to get the non-Indian world to recognize their people's contributions to America.

In a November 1991 interview, Wilma Mankiller, principal chief of the Cherokee Nation, said: "Overall, we have to encourage our people to look within our own history and culture and value system—our own communities and our families—for solutions to our problems." Winnemucca, who came to much the same conclusion in the 1860s, fought all her life for Indian self-determination and for recognition of Indian accomplishments. Contemporary Indians are still fighting that battle.

CHRONOLOGY

1844	Born Thocmetony in present-day Nevada
1850	Visits California; has first extensive contact with non-Indians
1857	Joins household of Major William M. Ormsby; learns English; adopts Christianity; becomes known as Sarah Winnemucca
1860	Briefly attends Catholic girls' school in California; three-month Pyramid Lake War takes place, resulting in the assignment of Paiutes to reservations
1864	Winnemucca makes stage appearances with father and sister in Virginia City, Nevada, and San Francisco, California
1865	Winnemucca's mother and 32 other Paiutes die in Mud Lake massacre
1867–68	Works as U. S. Army scout at Fort McDermit
1871	Marries army officer Edward C. Bartlett
1875	Becomes interpreter at Malheur Agency; serves as Paiute spokesperson; teaches school
1876	Divorces Bartlett; marries Joseph Satwaller; moves to Oregon
1878	Separates from Satwaller; becomes U.S. Army scout and guide during Bannock War; forced, with other Paiutes, into exile at Yakima reservation in Washington Territory
1879	Gives series of San Francisco lectures about Paiutes' plight
1880	Visits Washington, D.C., in vain effort to obtain aid for the Paiutes from Secretary of the Interior Carl Schurz
1881	Marries Lewis H. Hopkins in San Francisco
1882–83	Lectures in the Northeast; is befriended by writer-educators Mary Peabody Mann and Elizabeth Palmer Peabody
1883	Publishes *Life Among the Piutes*
1884	Appears before U.S. Congress to support federal aid to Paiutes
1885	Lectures in San Francisco; founds Peabody Indian School in Nevada; fails to obtain government support for school
1888	Closes Peabody Indian School; lives part-time with her sister Elma in Henry's Lake, Montana
1891	Dies at Henry's Lake on October 17

FURTHER READING

Brumble, H. David III. *American Indian Autobiography*. Berkeley: University of California Press, 1988.

Canfield, Gae Whitney. *Sarah Winnemuca of the Northern Paiutes*. Norman: University of Oklahoma Press, 1983.

Egan, Ferol. *Sand in a Whirlwind: The Paiute Indian War of 1860*. Garden City, NY: Doubleday, 1972.

Gehm, Katherine. *Sarah Winnemucca: Most Extraordinary Woman of the Paiute Nation*. Phoenix, AZ: O'Sullivan Woodside, 1975.

Hopkins, Sarah Winnemucca. *Life Among the Piutes*. Edited by Mrs. Horace Mann. New York: Putnam, 1883. Reprint. Bishop, CA: Chalfant Press, 1969.

Peabody, Elizabeth Palmer. *Sarah Winnemucca's Practical Solution to the Indian Problem*. Cambridge, MA: J. Wilson and Son, 1886.

INDEX

PICTURE CREDITS

ELLEN SCORDATO is the copy manager at an advertising agency in New York City and a freelance editor and writer. She graduated magna cum laude from Wellesley College with a B.A. in classical civilization.

W. DAVID BAIRD is the Howard A. White Professor of History at Pepperdine University in Malibu, California. He holds a Ph.D. from the University of Oklahoma and was formerly on the faculty of history at the University of Arkansas, Fayetteville, and Oklahoma State University. He has served as president of both the Western History Association, a professional organization, and Phi Alpha Theta, the international honor society for students of history. Dr. Baird is also the author of *The Quapaw Indians: A History of the Downstream People* and *Peter Pitchlynn: Chief of the Choctaws* and the editor of *A Creek Warrior of the Confederacy: The Autobiography of Chief G. W. Grayson.*

DUE DATE

MR 07 '00			
AP 11 '00			
	201-6503		Printed in USA